Cath Kidston®

SEWING BOOK

OVER 30 EXCLUSIVE PROJECTS MADE SIMPLE

PHOTOGRAPHY BY RITA PLATTS

Quadrille
PUBLISHING

CONTENTS

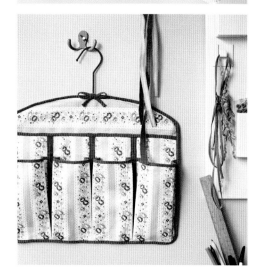

A NOTE FROM CATH

It's remarkable how sewing has become part of the mainstream over the last decade. Today, it's the stuff of prime-time TV and glossy magazines. Craft fairs and vintage markets are popping up all over the country, and all those old skills—like hand embroidery, upcycling, and patchwork—are coming back.

Five years on from my first sewing book, I wanted to follow up the huge success of *Sew!* with a very modern sewing book: practical, accessible, bright, and fun, with a breadth of projects that felt versatile and relevant for today.

Whatever your age, and regardless of whether you're a button-sewing novice or an expert with years of experience and shelves bursting with fabric, I hope this book inspires you to get stitching. All the basic techniques and paper patterns are explained at the front of the book and each project is paired with hand-drawn, step-by-step illustrations and beautiful photography, which means it's up to you how far you want to go.

If you're an absolute beginner, ease yourself in with some simple projects like the Envelope Purse (page 120) or Glasses Case (page 70), which can be accomplished in an hour or so, before stretching your skills with more challenging undertakings, such as the classic Holdall (page 110) or the Lunch Bag (page 132), or experimenting with different fabrics, from oilcloth to terry cloth to cotton seersucker.

Some projects will look really beautiful plain, others can be personalized with detailed embellishments, or adapted to fit your individual requirements, so this collection of basic sewing projects can become an endless resource for your own ideas.

For me, sewing is as much about the fabric as the making, so I've had a lot of fun choosing which prints and patterns to select for each project: I've used a variety of Cath Kidston® and vintage prints and plain fabrics in the designs, with trimmings and strong color contrasts playing a big role in creating that modern feel. The look is vintage inspired with a contemporary twist, a fresh palette, and some crisp details that will give your makes a professional finish.

One of my favorite projects is the Sewing Machine Cover (page 52) in retro flowers. I love how practical it is. If, like me, you like to sew at the kitchen table or at your desk, the last thing you want is to put your machine away mid-project. Our cover keeps everything perfectly under wraps and adds a cool, modern edge to the room.

I'm confident that, wherever you choose to set up your sewing, you will find all the ideas and guidance you need in these pages to take your skills to the next level and start creating something truly special!

SEWING BOX

Here's a guide to the basic equipment that you'll need in your sewing box. You'll find details of all of the fabric and any extra materials required for each project itemized in the Materials & Equipment list.

SCISSORS

Invest in high-quality steel blades that will last for a long time and can be sharpened if necessary. You will need three pairs:
- **EMBROIDERY SCISSORS** have narrow, pointed blades ideal for snipping thread, clipping seams, and cutting out small fabric shapes.
- **DRESSMAKER'S SHEARS** have long blades and an angled handle for accurate cutting out. Use for fabric only, as paper will dull the blades.
- **HOUSEHOLD SCISSORS** for interfacing, paper, and fusible adhesive web.
- **PINKING SHEARS** or **SCALLOP-EDGED SCISSORS** are useful but not essential. Zigzagged or scalloped edges reduce fraying along the edge of seams.

NEEDLES

These come in varying lengths and diameters. The size you use is a matter of personal preference, so start with a mixed selection. Store in the packet or a needlebook, as they can disappear inside a pincushion.
- **SHARPS** are medium-length needles with a small round eye and, as the name suggests, very sharp points. They are good for basting and general hand sewing.
- **CREWEL** or **EMBROIDERY NEEDLES** have longer, thinner eyes that can easily be threaded with cotton or wool embroidery threads.
- **QUILTING NEEDLES** are short, fine, and designed for hand quilting through layers of fabric and batting.
- **TAPESTRY NEEDLES** with blunt tips are used for needlepoint, but large ones are also very handy for threading elastic and cords.

THIMBLE

Worth wearing if you want to avoid punctured fingers when embroidering or hand sewing. Choose one that fits your finger snugly but not too tightly.

DRESSMAKER'S PINS

Long glass- or pearl-headed pins are easy to handle and show up well against patterned fabrics. If you are working with very fine cotton fabrics, choose slender steel pins, which won't make holes in the fabric. Keep your pins in a lidded box and use a small magnet to pick up strays, or make your own Tortoise Pincushion (page 60).

THREAD

Mercerized cotton sewing thread is designed for use on all natural fibers, so it's ideal for sewing cotton duck fabric or lightweight cotton fabrics. Keep a large spool of white in your sewing box, along with a spool of brightly colored thread for basting. Match your thread color to your fabric as closely as possible, but if you can't find an exact match, choose a slightly darker shade.

Embroidery floss comes in folded skeins, secured at both ends with paper bands. Pull on the loose end while holding onto one band to prevent the thread from tangling and cut off the length required. You can then separate out the six strands and use the number specified in the project.

MEASURING AND MARKING TOOLS

Look for a good-quality tape measure with metal tips, or one that winds itself into a holder. A short ruler is helpful for marking hems or seam allowances and a long clear quilter's ruler is essential for making paper pattern pieces. Keep a pair of compasses in your sewing box for drawing circle templates. For marking tools, make sure you have sharp pencils for making templates and for drawing appliqué shapes onto fusible web; traditional tailor's chalk for marking seam allowances and notches on fabric; and a fading fabric marker pen for drawing seam lines or quilting lines on fabric.

BASICS

SEWING MACHINES

All that you need to make any of the projects in this book is a solid basic machine that is robust enough for thicker fabric, maintains a regular tension, and gives you an even straight stitch and a zigzag. Any other extras are a bonus (although an automatic needle threader saves a lot of effort).

THE BASICS

All machines, however complex, work in the same way, by linking two threads. One of these lies on the surface of the fabric and the other below it, and they meet halfway to produce a lock stitch. The main reel of thread sits on a spindle at the top of the machine and then works its way through the arm of the machine and down to the needle, while the second thread is wound onto a small bobbin that lies below. If your machine is set at the correct tension, a line of stitching should look the same on both sides.

ANATOMY OF THE MACHINE

All modern machines have the same working parts and structure, however complex they may be. Read through the manufacturer's manual carefully to find out how to thread your machine and what all the various dials and levers are for.

• The **SPOOL PIN** is the spindle at the top right of the machine. Slide a spool of sewing thread onto this and, following the manual, take the thread along the arm and through the needle.

• The **BOBBIN WINDER** is also on the top of the arm. Use this rotating spindle to wind thread from a spool onto the round bobbins that hold the lower thread.

• The **TENSION ADJUSTER** alters the amount of pressure on the upper thread. Check that it's at the standard setting before stitching.

• The **NEEDLE** is screwed into the arm of the machine, just in front of the presser foot. As with sewing needles,

they come in different sizes. A "universal" or medium size 14/90 is fine for most projects, but you'll need a denim needle (size 16/100) for sewing dense fabrics like the canvas used for the bag on page 98.

• The **PRESSER FOOT** maintains pressure on the fabric as it passes under the needle. Some machines alter this pressure automatically according to the thickness of the fabric, but you may need to adjust it manually if you are using very thick or fine material. Use the lever on the side to move it up or down. Your machine will come with several interchangeable feet, of which the zipper foot is essential, and more are available for advanced stitching.

• The **THROAT PLATE**, on the flat bed of the machine, is pierced with a small round hole through which the tip of the needle passes and is engraved with a series of parallel lines that enable you to stitch with a regular seam allowance.

• The **FEED DOG** is the name given to the serrated ridges that you can see under the throat plate. These grip the fabric as they move up and down, and push it forward under the presser foot.

• The **BOBBIN CASE** lies under the main bed of the machine and contains the bobbin with the lower thread. The tension on this can be altered if necessary.

• The **FOOT PEDAL** is your accelerator: the harder you press, the faster the machine will go, but many sewing machines have separate speed dials, which means that there's no fear of it all running away with you.

GETTING STARTED

The majority of the projects in this book are made up from basic geometric shapes such as squares, rectangles, and circles. The exact dimensions for each piece are given in the Cutting Out lists, with the width always appearing first, then the length.

PAPER PATTERNS

You can make your own paper patterns by marking the Cutting Out measurements on a sheet of pattern paper. This comes ready printed with a square grid of lines every quarter inch or dots every inch, so all you have to do is draw and cut along the guides (see Resources on page 160). Unless stated in the instructions, the pattern-piece sizes include all the seam allowances. The diameter of any circular pieces is also given in the Cutting Out list, so halve this number to find the radius and use a pair of compasses and a pencil to draw the pattern.

TEMPLATES

The more complex shapes are given as templates and you'll find these at the back of the book. All are actual size, which means you can trace or photocopy them to make your own paper patterns. Transfer any markings on the templates—the Crocodile's eye and mouth (page 159), for example—onto the fabric using a fading fabric marker pen or chalk pencil.

CUTTING LAYOUTS

Many of the project instructions provide cutting layouts at the start of the project. Like the diagram on a dressmaking pattern, these show which pattern pieces you need and the best way of arranging them on your fabric. The double-headed arrows on the layouts indicate which way up the pattern pieces should be, so that they follow the grain, or straight threads, of the fabric.

ROTARY CUTTING

An alternative method of cutting out is to use a long, wide, clear quilter's ruler marked with a grid, a rotary cutter (choose one with a retractable blade for safety), and a large cutting mat. These enable you to cut squares, strips, and rectangles speedily and accurately: it's well worth investing in all three items if you are going to do a lot of sewing.

PREPARING THE FABRIC

The fabric quantities given in the Materials & Equipment list are always larger than the minimum amount required, but if you are using a large-scale print or stripes, you may need to allow a little extra so that you can match up the pattern across the pieces.

Dressmakers always launder their fabric before starting work, to allow for any shrinkage and to remove the dressings used in the manufacturing process, but unless you're going to make the Scallop-Edged Pillowcase (page 24) or the Baby Gift Set (page 146) you won't need to do this.

Do give your fabric a good press before cutting out though, to remove any fold marks. A silicone or starch spray is useful for getting rid of stubborn creases. If you're upcycling vintage fabric, however, it is a good idea to wash it first, to make sure that it's robust enough to stand up to everyday use and that the colors won't run. Avoid any holes or rustmarks and areas that have faded or worn thin over the years.

SEAMS & HEMS

The most basic skills—sewing seams and hems—involve joining two pieces of fabric together and finishing the raw edges. Once you have learned how to do these neatly and accurately, you should be able to make any of the projects in this book.

SEAMS

Careful preparation always ensures professional-looking results, so take time to pin and baste each seam before you sew. Follow the instructions carefully, as they tell you how to prepare your fabric and will give details of the individual seam allowances. For some projects, you will have to bind the raw edges or finish them with a zigzag or overlocking stitch before sewing the seams to prevent the fabric from fraying, but the instructions will always tell you when to do this. It's a good idea to reinforce both ends of each seam with a few stitches worked in the opposite direction, to prevent the two threads from unraveling. Check your sewing machine manual to find the reverse/backstitch lever, or to see if it has a function that will do this automatically.

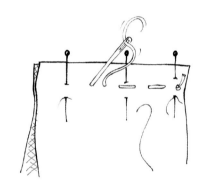

SEAM ALLOWANCE

This is the distance between the edge of the fabric and the stitching line, and it varies depending on the project and the type of fabric you are using. You'll find a series of parallel lines engraved on the throat plate of your sewing machine: pick the one marked with the measurement you need and keep the edge of the fabric aligned to this as you stitch.

PINNING AND BASTING

Place the two pieces of fabric together, with the right sides facing inward. Match up the corners, align the raw edges, and pin the two layers together. Insert the pins at right angles, at intervals of 2" to 6" [5 to 15 cm], depending on the length of the seam. Baste (see page 19) just inside the seam line, then take out the pins. Remember to remove the basting after machine stitching the seam.

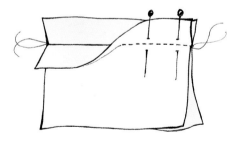

STRAIGHT SEAM

Lift up the machine's presser foot and slide the top end of the fabric underneath. Line up the right-hand raw edge with the correct guideline on the throat plate and lower the foot. Lower the needle and sew to the end of the seam. Raise the needle and the presser foot and lift out the fabric. Trim the threads.

PRESSING

Every seam has to be pressed flat. The step instructions tell you when to do this and whether the allowance should be pressed open (a), inward (b), or to one side (c). Right-angled or curved seams need to be trimmed before the piece is turned right-side out: see opposite.

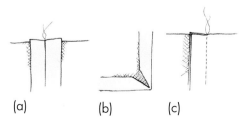

(a)   (b)   (c)

CORNER SEAM

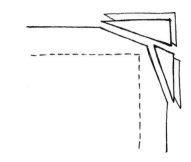

You'll need this technique for the pillows (pages 32 and 36), Book Cover (page 124), and Zip-Up Pouches (page 66). Stitch along the first edge and stop when you reach the corner point. With the needle still down, lift the presser foot and turn the fabric through 90 degrees. Lower the foot and sew along the second edge. Trim two small triangles from the seam allowance, to reduce the bulk. Turn the fabric right-side out, carefully ease out the corner with a knitting needle, then press.

T-JUNCTION SEAM

This smart seam gives depth to a bag. It's one of my favorite finishes and appears on the terry-cloth Wash Bag (page 82) and Handbag (page 94). Stitch the side and bottom seams, leaving the cut-out corners unstitched. Press the seams open. Refold the corners, lining up the seams, and pin them together. Machine stitch along the given seam allowance, then trim the seam and finish with a zigzag stitch or binding.

CURVED SEAM

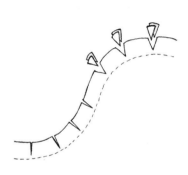

The Scallop-Edged Pillowcase (page 24) is undoubtedly the best way to perfect this technique, but there are also outside curves on the Fold-Up Tray (page 44). Pin, baste, and machine stitch as above, keeping the seam allowance regular as you guide the fabric under the presser foot. You will need to cut into this seam allowance before turning right-side out to create a smooth seam line. For an inside curve (left), make a series of small snips at right angles to the seam line, so that the seam allowance will stretch out. Cut to within 1/16" [2 mm] of the stitches. On an outward curve (right), snip regularly spaced triangular notches, so that the seam allowance will fit comfortably within the curve.

SEWING A CIRCLE TO A CYLINDER

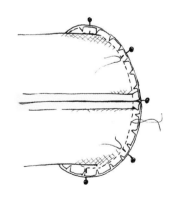

This three-dimensional seam is used when you need to sew a round base onto a tube of fabric, as on the Yoga Mat Bag (page 102), Gym Bag (page 106), and Bottle Holder (page 146). To make sure it all fits together neatly, fold the circle in half, then quarters and eighths, and mark each of the eight equal divisions with a pin. Cut a round of 1/4" [6 mm] snips into the seam allowance of the cylinder, spacing them about 3/4" [2 cm] apart. Fold into eight divisions and mark them with pins. Pin the two pieces with right sides together and with the marker pins aligned. Baste just inside the seam allowance, then machine stitch with the cylinder uppermost. You may then need to clip into the seam allowance on the circle for a neat finish, depending on the thickness of the fabric.

TOPSTITCHED SEAM

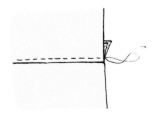

Topstitching is used to give extra strength and a decorative finish to a seam, as on the Holdall pockets (page 110). Press the seam allowance to one side. With the right-side uppermost, sew through all three layers of fabric, machine stitching closely parallel to the seam line.

HEMS

There are two ways to finish a raw edge. You can fold it over to the back of the fabric and stitch it down to make a flat hem, but a more decorative method is to bind it with a narrow strip of fabric or with ready-made bias binding. There are two types of hem—single and double. A single hem has just one turning and is used for items like the Tissue Box Cover (page 28) or the Sewing Machine Cover (page 52) where the back of the fabric will be hidden from view. A double hem is folded over twice to give a firm, reversible edge, as seen on the Tote (page 90) and Handbag (page 94). The depth of the turnings is always specified in the instructions.

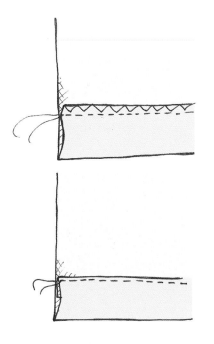

SINGLE HEM
Zigzag or overlock stitch the edge of the fabric. Then with the right side facing downward, fold edge to the wrong side. Use a tape measure or ruler to make sure that the turning is a consistent depth all the way along, then press, baste, or pin it in place, as instructed. Machine stitch the hem, using the guidelines on the throat plate to keep the line straight.

DOUBLE HEM
Fold and press the first turning as for the single hem, then turn it under a second time to the given depth. Baste through all the layers, then machine stitch 1/8" [4 mm] from the inner fold.

BINDING
A bound edge always gives a neat, "finished" look to a project, and using a contrasting color gives definition to the outline and any pockets. I chose bright pinks to bind the Hanging Organizer (page 40) and the Pocket Sewing Kit (page 74) but went for a matching pale blue for the Baby Gift Set (page146). Binding can also be used to finish bulky inside seams, unobtrusively, with matching bias binding as on the Laptop Case (page 84) or decoratively, as for the open seams on the Canvas Bag (page 98), which are finished off with narrow strips of vintage fabric.

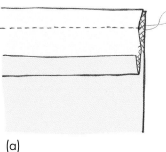

(a)

BINDING A STRAIGHT EDGE

If you are using bias binding, start by opening out the fold along one edge. With right sides together, baste this edge to the edge of the fabric or along the seam allowance. Machine stitch along the first fold (a). If you are binding with a straight-grain fabric strip—as for the Canvas Bag (page 98)—prepare the strip with pressed folds. First fold the strip in half lengthwise and press. Then open out and fold each long edge to the center and press. Stitch on along one long edge as explained for the bias binding.

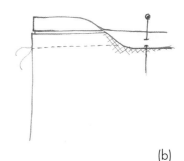

(b)

Next, fold the remaining folded edge of the binding to the right side so that the raw edges are enclosed (b). Baste and machine stitch close to the fold or slip-stitch the folded edge by hand (see page 19).

BOUND CURVES

This is how the scallops on the baby's Towel (page 152) and curved corners of the Envelope Purse (page 120) are finished off. As above, open out the binding and, with right sides together, baste it to the edge of the fabric (c). You will need to stretch out the raw edges slightly and ease in the center fold as you go round the curve, so that the binding will fit comfortably over the edge of the fabric without pulling it inward.

(c)

Turn the binding to the wrong side of the fabric. Ease out and slip-stitch the folded edge (d). Gently steam press the binding for a neat curve.

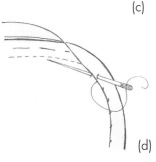

(d)

BOUND RIGHT-ANGLED CORNERS

Baste the binding in place as above, until the distance from the corner is the same as the depth of the first turning—usually about 1/4" [6 mm]. Make a 45-degree fold, so that the raw edge now lies alongside the next edge, and continue basting. Machine stitch along the fold.

Finish off by turning the binding to the back and refold the creases. Tuck under the surplus binding on both sides to make a neatly mitered corner.

BOUND INSIDE CORNERS

You'll need this technique for the baby's Towel (page 152), at the points where the scallops meet. Baste the open edge of the binding along the first curve, easing the outside edge to fit, and ending directly below the inside angle. Pleat the binding so that the raw edge lies along the next curve. Continue to the end and machine stitch along the fold line, taking care not to catch the binding. Turn the folded edge over to the back and baste it in place, once again pleating the surplus fabric at the inside corners. Use the point of your embroidery scissors to push the pleat under the binding for neat angles. Sew down by hand or machine.

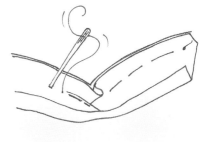

EMBROIDERY & HAND STITCHES

There are literally hundreds of different embroidery stitches you can use to embellish your fabric creations. To get you started, here are the stitches that appear on the two pillow covers (pages 32 and 36).

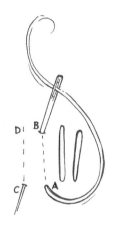

STRAIGHT STITCH

Use this as a decorative edging around appliqué shapes and for small highlights of color and short lines. Simply bring the needle up at A and take it down again at the top of the line, at B. Make the next stitch from C up to D.

SATIN STITCH

This stitch has a smooth, silky appearance. It consists of a row of straight stitches, worked closely together within a given outline. Make a stitch from A to B, then bring the needle out at C, a thread's width to the left, ready for the next straight stitch.

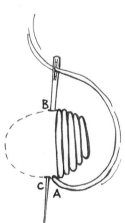

FLY STITCH

The ideal stitch for leaves. Start with a short straight stitch at the top, then fill in the outline with closely spaced Y-shaped stitches. Bring the needle up at A and down at B. Pull it through over the thread at C and take it back down at D to make an anchor stitch.

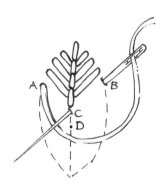

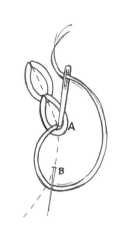

CHAIN STITCH

These interlinked looped stitches are ideal for stitching intricate shapes and lettering. Take the needle down at A and loop the thread from left to right. Bring the needle back up at B and draw it through over the thread. Carefully pull up the thread to make a small loop, then continue along the marked line, starting the next loop at B.

BACKSTITCH

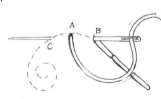

This stitch can be used for hand-sewn seams and for "drawing" fine lines within an embroidered design. Come up at A and make a backward stitch to B. Bring the needle out again at C, a stitch length from A, then continue to the end of the line. If you are stitching along a tight curve, you will need to make smaller stitches.

INTERLACED CHAIN STITCH

A composite stitch worked in two colors, this is sewn along the horizontal seam line on the Mushroom Pillow (page 32). Start with a row of chain stitches, then thread a blunt-tipped needle with a contrasting thread. Bring it up by the first stitch and slide up upward, under the second stitch. Slide it down under the third, then continue weaving behind the chain stitches to make a wavy line.

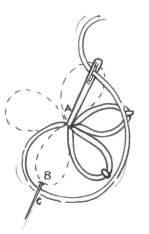

LAZY DAISY STITCH

This is the obvious choice for embroidering flowers and petals. It is made up of individual chain stitches that all start at the same center point. Chain stitch from A to B, as above, then take the needle through at C, making a short straight stitch to anchor the loop. Sew more "petals" to complete the flower.

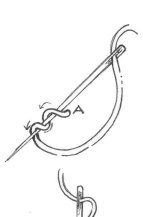

FRENCH KNOTS

These tiny round knots are used for highlights of color and for flower centers. They take a little bit of practice. Bring the needle up at A and wind the thread twice around the tip in an counterclockwise direction. Maintaining tension on the thread with your other hand so that the loops don't slip off, take the needle through close to A, at B, and draw it gently through the loops.

Most of the seams and hems used in the projects are machine stitched, but there are two useful hand techniques that you will need to know.

BASTING

These long, evenly spaced stitches are used to hold two pieces of fabric together temporarily. Use a contrasting color of thread so that the basting shows up well, and secure the end of the seam with a double stitch. Clip, then remove the basting thread after the seam has been machine stitched.

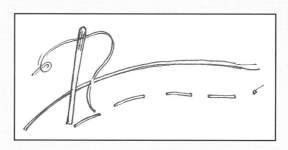

SLIP STITCH

This produces an almost invisible join between two pieces of fabric and is used to close the opening between two folded edges, such as an opening in the lining of a bag. Bring the needle up from inside the lower fold and insert it into the fold directly above. Slip the needle through the fold and come out again, $1/16$" to $1/4$" [2 to 6 mm] to the left. Take a short stitch through the first fold in the same way. Repeat this to the end.

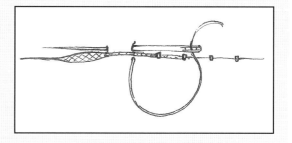

FASTENINGS

Fastenings need to be functional and secure, but they can also be decorative. Look out for neon zippers, pretty vintage buttons, and bakelite buckles to use alongside more practical magnetic bag fasteners, spring clips, and drawstring cords.

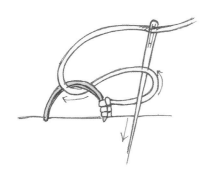

BUTTONHOLE LOOP

This traditional dressmaking finish is used for the buttonhole loop on the Pocket Sewing Kit (page 74). Make a foundation bar of two loose stitches and cover it with a row of tailor's buttonhole stitch, starting at the bottom right. For each stitch, pass the needle from right to left under the bar and then down through the loop of thread on the right, making sure that the top part of the loop lies above the needle, as shown. Gently draw up the thread so that it forms a small purl that lies parallel to the bar. Repeat this to the end of the bar to form a semicircular loop.

ZIPPERS

Adding a zipper to a pencil case, laptop cover, or bag isn't nearly as complicated as inserting one into a garment, where it may need to be concealed with a flap or set invisibly into a seam. I like to use zippers as a way to add stripes of bright color to a project. If you look at the Zip-Up Pouches (page 66), you'll see how the neon pink lifts the floral prints. Detailed instructions are given for each of the projects that has a zipper, and with careful and secure basting plus some slow, steady machine stitching you shouldn't have any problems. Zippers are made of two tapes, each edged with a line of metal or plastic teeth, which open up or interlock when the pull is moved. Baste the edge of your fabric securely to the tape before stitching and always fit the correct narrow zipper foot to your machine. This enables you to stitch close to the teeth, so be sure to check that the needle is in the correct position before you start to sew. You can find out how to do this in your machine manual. Use a thread to match the fabric and reinforce both ends of each seam with a few backstitches.

When you are sewing, keep the needle a constant distance from the teeth. Just before you reach the zipper pull, raise the presser foot, keeping the needle in the down position. Gently slide the pull backward, behind the needle. Lower the foot again and continue stitching to the end. Take care not to stitch into the tabs that join the two sides of the zipper.

HOOK-AND-LOOP TAPE

This quick and practical fastening, also called touch-and-close tape, is especially suited to children's items like the Lunch Bag (page132) or the Terry-Cloth Bib (page 150). Hook-and-loop tape can be bought by length or as small round dots, sometimes called "coins." One side is covered with dense loops and the other with small hooks: when they meet, they form a strong bond. Separate out the two sides. Sew the looped side to the bottom layer and the hooked side to the top layer of your project. Stitch carefully around the outside edge with thread to match the main fabric.

STRAPS & HANDLES

A well-chosen handle is the finishing touch for any bag. Depending on the style, I like to use sturdy cotton tape, which comes in a range of colors, thicknesses, and different weaves, or fabric handles made in either matching or contrasting material. The Eye Mask (page 78) has an elasticated strap made from a tube of fabric. Without the elastic, this type of narrow strap would be a good alternative to a ribbon handle for the Envelope Purse (page 120).

FLAT HANDLE

To make a flat handle for a bag, cut a strip $3/4$" [2 cm] wider than the finished width and $3/4$" [2 cm] longer than the required length. Press under a $3/8$" [1 cm] turning along each long edge, then press in half lengthwise. Unfold and press under a $3/8$" [1 cm] turning at both short ends. Refold, then baste the folded edges together and topstitch close to the outside edge all the way around, using matching thread.

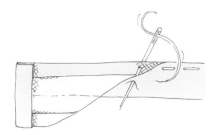

REINFORCING STITCHES

When you sew a handle onto a bag, you need to "box stitch"—that is, sew a square of reinforcing stitches at the end, so that the main bag won't tear. First, baste the end of the handle securely in position. Then, starting at the top right corner, stitch an open square through the bag and handle, sewing over the existing stitching lines on the handle. Sew diagonally across to the bottom left corner, along the bottom edge, then diagonally up to the top left corner. Finish off with a second line of stitches along the top edge. You may find it helpful to draw the square and lines on first. Using the reverse lever to sew backward will save you having to move the fabric about under the presser foot.

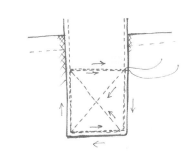

NARROW STRAP

Fold the fabric strip in half lengthwise, right sides together, and pin the raw edges together. Machine stitch along the long edge, about $1/4$" to $3/8$" [6 to 10 mm] from the edge, depending on the thickness of the fabric. Slant the end of the seam out to the corner. Trim back the seam allowance to $1/8$" [4 mm]. Thread a blunt-tipped tapestry needle with a short length of strong thread, fasten it to the corner, and tie the ends together. Pass the needle slowly through the tube: the fabric will gradually turn right-side out as it is turned through. You can also use a safety pin for turning through wider tubes and serious stitchers may have a rouleaux turner, a special long thin tool with a latchet hook at one end.

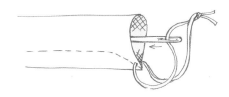

HOME

Easy

SCALLOP-EDGED PILLOWCASE

A simple take on a classic shape. Sewing your own pillowcase is a very straightforward process, even one with a scalloped edge like this. The border is made up of shallow, continuous curves. As you'll be using a fine fabric, you can easily create a smooth edge by trimming the seam allowance right back, instead of clipping into the curves as you would do with anything thicker.

MATERIALS & EQUIPMENT

TEMPLATE ON PAGES 154–155

42" x 51" [110 x 130 cm] of a lightweight cotton print
Matching sewing thread
Sheet of paper 35" x 27" [89 x 64 cm]
Sewing box (see page 8)
Sewing machine

SIZE

To fit a 20" x 30" [50 x 76 cm]
queen-size pillow

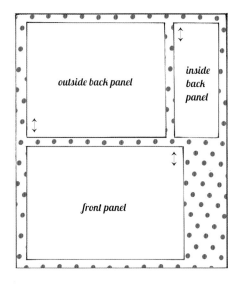

CUTTING OUT

Remember to launder and press new fabric before cutting out, to allow for any shrinkage.

- One 33 1/2" x 24 1/2" [85 x 62 cm] front panel
- One 29 1/2" x 24 1/2" [75 x 62 cm] outside back panel
- One 10" x 24 1/2" [25 x 62 cm] inside back panel

FABRIC CHOICE

Use a fine fabric with a high thread count. I recycled this red and white polka dot from a summer scarf, but any 100% cotton would work. Old sheets have a wonderfully soft quality that comes from years of use and laundering, and recycled into pillowcases they make great presents.

tip... USE PLENTY OF PINS AT EVERY STAGE OF MAKING THE PILLOWCASE, TO KEEP THE LAYERS OF FINE FABRIC FROM SHIFTING.

TO MAKE THE PILLOWCASE

DRAW THE PAPER PATTERN PIECE

The template on pages 154 to 155 is just one quarter of the front panel. Fold a 35" x 27" [90 x 70 cm] sheet of paper in half lengthwise and then in half widthwise to divide it into four. Unfold the creases. Place the template in each quarter in turn and draw around the curved edge, adjusting the position so that the straight edges always line up with the crease lines. Cut out around the outside edge.

PREPARE THE PANELS

01 Pin the paper pattern centrally to the wrong side of the front panel and draw around the scalloped edge with a fading fabric marker pen. Press and stitch a double ³/8" [1 cm] hem along one short edge of the outside back panel and along one long edge of the inside back panel.

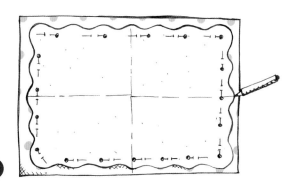

PIN THE LAYERS TOGETHER

Lay the front panel right-side up on your work surface. Lay the outside back panel right-side down across the left-hand end, matching the raw edges carefully.

02 Lay the inside back panel right-side down across the right-hand end, so that the hems overlap. Pin the three pieces together around the outside edge, with the pins parallel to the edges.

SEW THE SCALLOPS

03 Turn the whole thing over and insert a second round of pins, positioning them ³/4" [2 cm] inside

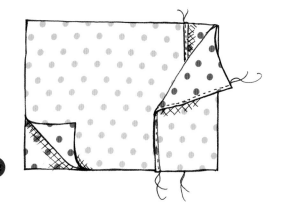

the wavy outline. Carefully stitch the front and back panels together along the marked line, following the scallops precisely.

04 Trim the seam allowance back to ¹/₈" [4 mm] all around, following the curves. Turn the pillowcase right-side out and ease out the curves, rolling the fabric between your fingers so that the seam lies at the outside edge. Press the border lightly.

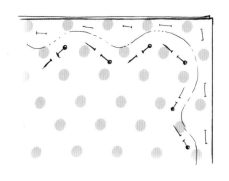
03

STITCH THE INNER RECTANGLE

05 Using a long quilter's ruler and a fading fabric marker pen, draw a rectangle on the front of the pillowcase, positioning it about ³/₄" [2 cm] in from the innermost point of the curves as shown on the template. Pin the front and back together ³/₄" [2 cm] from the line, then work a line of basting ¹/₄" [6 mm] away from the line. Machine stitch along the rectangular outline to complete the pillowcase.

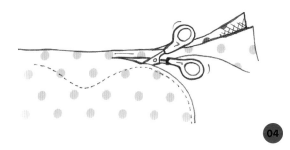
04

TAKE IT FURTHER

If you want to make an Oxford pillowcase with a plain border, simply omit the scallops. Pin the pieces together as in diagram 02, but then stitch around the outside edge, taking a ³/₈" [1 cm] seam allowance. Clip the corners and turn right-side out, then mark and stitch the inner rectangle to the pillow size.

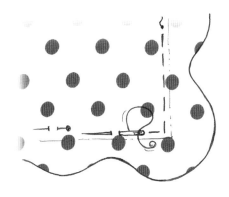
05

Easy

TISSUE BOX COVER

This may be simple enough to run up within an hour, but it's also very practical. Working out the measurements for the templates introduces some basic pattern-cutting skills, so it's also a useful learning project.

MATERIALS & EQUIPMENT

Approximately 32" x 8" [80 x 20 cm] of a medium-weight cotton print

Matching sewing thread

Sewing pattern paper or quilter's graph paper

Sewing box (see page 8)

Sewing machine

CUTTING OUT

Measure your box and make the paper patterns to cut these pieces (see right).

- Two main panels
- Two end panels

MAKE THE PAPER PATTERNS

Tailor this cover to fit your own tissue box by doing some simple math. Start by measuring the width (W), depth (D), and height (H) and make a note of each. The two main panels each measure W + $1\frac{1}{4}$" [3 cm] by H + $\frac{1}{2}$ D + $1\frac{1}{4}$" [3 cm]. The end panels measure W + $1\frac{1}{4}$" [3 cm] by D + $1\frac{1}{4}$" [3 cm]. Draw the shapes on sewing pattern paper or quilter's graph paper and cut out a template for each of the four pieces.

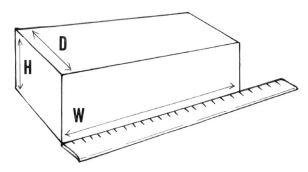

FABRIC CHOICE

The rectangular shape of the cover works well with a strong print, like this vintage curtain fabric, but take care with print direction and pattern repeat, as it looks best when the design on the panels matches up.

tip... MAKE YOUR TEMPLATES FIRST TO WORK OUT EXACTLY HOW MUCH FABRIC YOU WILL NEED. WHEN YOU ARE CUTTING THEM OUT, TAKE CARE TO LINE UP THE TOP EDGE OF EACH PIECE ALONG THE SAME PART OF THE PRINTED DESIGN.

TO MAKE THE TISSUE BOX COVER

PREPARE THE FABRIC PANELS

Finish the side and top edges of each panel with an overlocking or zigzag stitch. Using a fading fabric marker pen and a ruler, mark a $^5/_8$" [1.5 cm] seam line along the wrong side of the top and side edges of the end panels and along the side edges of the main panels.

STITCH AROUND THE OPENING

01 Pin the two main panels right sides together along the top edge. Mark 2" [5 cm] in from each corner with a pin. Taking a $^5/_8$" [1.5 cm] seam allowance, sew between the corners and the pins. (You may need to make these seams a little longer, depending on the proportions of your box.)

02 Press the seam allowance open, including on either side of the opening. Stitching from the right side, sew all the way around the opening, $^1/_4$" [6 mm] from the pressed-under edge. Double stitch over the short ends of the opening for extra strength.

COMPLETE THE COVER

03 Fold an end panel in half widthwise and insert a pin at the center of the top edge. With right sides together, pin this point to the seam at one edge of the main piece, then pin the bottom corners together on each side. Baste the two pieces together, just inside the marked seam line, starting at the center seam and working outward in each direction. When you reach each top corner make a $^3/_8$" [1 cm] snip into the main panel at this point, so that the fabric will fold neatly around the corner.

Machine stitch along the marked seam line, with the main panel uppermost. At each corner, lift the presser foot, leaving the needle down, pivot the fabric 90 degrees, and continue stitching.

Join on the other end panel in the same way. Trim a small triangle from the top corner of each end panel, then press all the seams open. Zigzag or overlock stitch all around the bottom edge. Turn up a $^5/_8$" [1.5 cm] hem, then baste and machine stitch. Turn the cover right-side out, press, and slip it over the box.

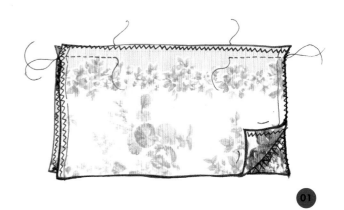

MUSHROOM PILLOW

This rectangular pillow cover, with its bright appliqué mushrooms, is made from a mixture of four polka dot prints, each one a different scale. More color is added with some simple embroidery, which makes it an ideal sampler if you're learning how to sew: straight stitch around the outside edges, with extra satin stitch dots to add texture, lazy daisy and chain stitch for the flowers, and a textured band of interlaced chain stitch along the seam line.

MATERIALS & EQUIPMENT

TEMPLATES ON PAGES 158–159

22" x 18" [55 x 45 cm] of a dark green polka
  dot cotton duck fabric
18" x 10" [45 x 25 cm] of unbleached linen
6" [15 cm] square each of taupe, turquoise, red,
  and pink polka dot cotton duck fabric, for the appliqué
18" x 8" [45 x 20 cm] of fusible adhesive web
Six-strand embroidery floss in taupe, turquoise, red, pink,
  lemon, dark green, medium blue, and grass green
Matching sewing threads
16" x 12" [40 x 30 cm] pillow form
Sewing box (see page 8)
Sewing machine

SIZE

To fit 16" x 12" [40 x 30 cm] pillow form

CUTTING OUT

FROM LINEN
- One 16" x 9" [40 x 23 cm] main front panel

FROM GREEN POLKA DOT COTTON DUCK FABRIC
- One 16" x 3¹/2" [40 x 9 cm] lower front strip
- Two 10" x 12" [25 x 30 cm] back panels

FABRIC CHOICE

This kind of appliqué works well if you use different textures of fabric. An old plain linen dishtowel would make a great base for the main front panel.

TAKE IT FURTHER *These adaptable mushrooms look great together, but they work just as well singly. Appliqué just one onto a plain calico tote or a baby blanket, or sew a whole row along the hem of a nursery curtain.*

MAKE IT SIMPLER

Hand embroidery gives a unique look to the appliqué: for a more speedy finish, you could try edging the shapes with a machine zigzag or satin stitch in matching thread.

TO MAKE THE PILLOW COVER

PREPARE THE PILLOW FRONT

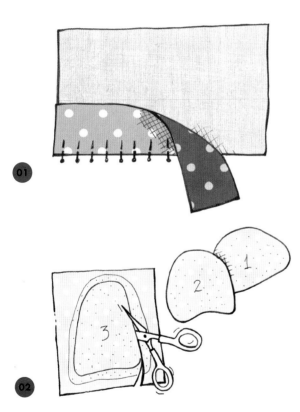

01 Place the green lower front strip across the bottom edge of the linen main front panel, with the right sides together. Pin, then machine stitch, taking a ³/₈" [1 cm] seam allowance. Press the seam allowance to the side so that it lies over the polka dot fabric.

APPLIQUÉ THE MUSHROOMS

Trace the full-size mushroom templates from pages 158 to 159 onto the paper side of the fusible adhesive web, numbering each of the six individual shapes. Cut them out roughly, about ¹/₂" [12 mm] outside the outlines.

02 With the adhesive side down, press the pieces of fusible adhesive web onto the wrong side of the polka dot appliqué fabrics: the three stalks go on the taupe fabric, top 1 on turquoise, top 2 on red, and top 3 on pink. Cut each shape out carefully around the pencil outline.

03 Peel off the backing papers. Arrange the stalks across the linen panel, from 1 to 3, and add the mushroom tops. Check that there is at least ³/₄" [2 cm] between the shapes and the outer edge of the linen. When you are happy with the layout, press the shapes in place, using a cloth to protect the surface of the iron.

ADD THE EMBROIDERY

04 Draw in the extra ovals around the mushroom tops with a fading fabric marker pen. Using three strands of matching embroidery floss, edge the mushroom tops with small straight stitches (see page 18). Keep the stitches roughly the same size—about 1¹/₂" [4 cm] long—and space them evenly apart, at right angles to the edge.

05 When you reach the ovals, fill these in with satin stitch (page 18), altering the length of the stitches to fit the shapes. Edge the stalks with straight stitches, using three strands of taupe embroidery floss.

06 Finish off by drawing in the flower stems at the base of the mushrooms. Sew over each one in chain stitch, using three strands of dark green floss. Using six strands of thread and referring to the photo on page 33 for the colors, work the flowers in lazy daisy stitch with a French knot at the center of each one. Sew a line of chain stitch on the linen right next to the seam line above the green lower front strip in pink and interlace it with grass green, using six strands of floss. You can see how to work all the embroidery stitches on pages 18 to 19.

COMPLETE THE PILLOW COVER

07 Finish one 12" [30 cm] edge of each back panel with a ³/₈" [1 cm] single hem. With right sides together, place one panel across the pillow front, matching the top, bottom, and right-hand edges. Pin it in place, then pin the other panel to the left-hand side.

Machine stitch all the way around the pillow cover, taking a ³/₈" [1 cm] seam allowance. Clip a triangle from each corner, snipping to within ³/₈" [1 cm] of the stitches, and turn the cover right-side out. Ease out the seams, press lightly, and insert the pillow form.

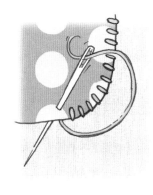
04

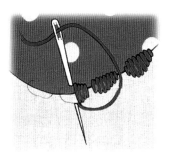
05

06

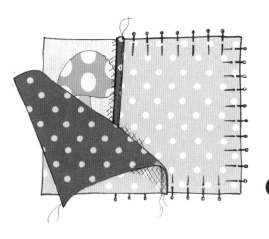
07

tip... IF YOU ARE A BEGINNER, BASTE THE BACK PANELS TO THE FRONT AND REMOVE THE PINS BEFORE MACHINE STITCHING THEM TOGETHER.

Easy

EMBROIDERED PILLOW

Embroidery can be rather a painstaking process, so this pillow is ideal for anybody with limited stitching time. All you have to do is to choose your favorite design areas within the patterned background fabric, then sew over the outlines with matching floss, giving you maximum visual impact for minimal preparation! Every version will be individual, so you can really put your own personal stamp on this project.

MATERIALS & EQUIPMENT

20" x 20" [50 x 50 cm] of a medium-weight cotton print, for the front

22" x 16" [55 x 40 cm] of a cotton polka dot or other contrasting medium-weight fabric, for the back panels

Six-strand embroidery floss in colors to match front fabric

Matching sewing thread

60" [150 cm] of ready-made piping cord, with a $^3/_8$" [1 cm] seam allowance

14" x 14" [35.5 x 35.5 cm] pillow form

Embroidery hoop (optional)

Sewing box (see page 8)

Sewing machine

SIZE

To fit 14" x 14" [35 x 35 cm] pillow form

CUTTING OUT

FROM BACK-PANEL FABRIC

• Two 10" x 14$^1/_2$" [25 x 37 cm] back panels

FABRIC CHOICE

I used my Brighton-inspired Brighten Up Your Day print here, but any print with strong outlines to embroider will work.

TO MAKE THE PILLOW COVER

MARK THE PILLOW FRONT

Draw a 14$^3/_4$" [37 cm] square on the patterned front fabric, picking an area that contains an interesting part of the design. Don't cut this out yet, as you will need some spare fabric around the outside edge when you are stitching close to the outline. Mount the area to be stitched in an embroidery hoop, if you wish.

EMBROIDER THE OUTLINES

You can find out how to work the basic embroidery stitches on pages 18 to 19, although you may have some favorites of your own to add.

01 Backstitch is good for curvy lines, so use this to embroider over some of the handwritten text. For a very curvy and looped outline like this, the stitches will need to be about $^1/_8$" [4 mm] long.

TAKE IT FURTHER

Why not add embroidered detail to your other projects in the same way? You could pick out one of the birds from the Tote Bag (page 90) or a flower from the Handbag (page 94). Match your threads to the colors in the fabric so that the motifs blend in, or go for a bright contrast to make them stand out.

tip... IF YOU WANT BOLD STITCHES, SEW WITH ALL SIX STRANDS OF THE EMBROIDERY THREAD AND A LARGE-EYED NEEDLE. FOR FINER STITCHES, SEPARATE OUT THE STANDS AND USE JUST THREE AT A TIME.

02 Work chain stitch around the flowers, as this produces a thicker outline. Working each petal individually, rather than going all the way around in a continuous line, will give you a more accurate shape. You can also use chain stitch for straight lines, such as the edges of the postcards.

FILL IN THE LEAVES

03 Fly stitch, with its pattern of chevrons, is good for leaves. Use green thread and vary the width of each individual stitch so that it fits within the outline. Start and finish each stitch at the center of the leaf to make a "vein." Work straight stitches over the stalks.

ADD HIGHLIGHTS

04 French knots are perfect for small dots of color. Use these to fill in the centers of the flowers.

COMPLETE THE COVER

05 When you have finished, press then trim the embroidered front piece to 14¾" [37 cm] square, along the drawn outline. Lay it out with the right side facing upward. Starting close to one corner, baste the piping cord all the way around the outside, aligning the inside edge of the cord ⅜" [1 cm] from the edge of the fabric. Make a small snip into the tape at each corner. Overlap the cord ends and then trim them in line with the fabric edge.

06 Finish one long edge of each back panel with a double ⅜" [1 cm] hem. With the right sides facing inward, pin one panel to the left-hand side of the pillow front, matching the raw edges. Pin the other panel to the right-hand side.

Using a zipper foot so that you can stitch close to the piping cord, machine stitch around the outside edge, taking a ⅜" [1 cm] seam allowance.

Clip the corners to reduce the bulk (see page 15) and turn the cover right-side out. Ease out the seams and corners, then press lightly. Insert the pillow form.

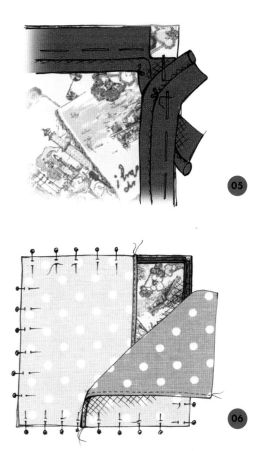

05

06

tip... YOU MAY NEED TO WASH YOUR PILLOW COVER ONE DAY, SO REMEMBER THAT COTTON DUCK HAS A SHRINKAGE RATE OF 5%. WASH AND PRESS THE FABRIC AND PIPING BEFORE YOU CUT THEM OUT AND DOUBLE CHECK THAT YOUR EMBROIDERY THREADS ARE COLORFAST.

HANGING ORGANIZER

Storage always seems to be at a premium, so this hanging tidy is an excellent way to provide extra space for bottles, brushes, and soap in the bathroom, utensils in the kitchen, or cleaning products.

MATERIALS & EQUIPMENT

55" x 20" [140 x 50 cm] of a medium-weight cotton print with stripes (you may need extra to match up the pattern repeat)

[4$^1/_2$ yards [4 m] of bias binding, $^5/_8$" [15 mm] wide

Sewing thread to match bias binding

13" [33 cm] curved wooden coat hanger

Sewing box (see page 8)

Sewing machine

SIZE

Approximately 14$^3/_4$" x 16" [36 x 40 cm]

MAKE IT SIMPLER

Replace the folded pockets with a single 16$^1/_2$" x 10" [42 x 25 cm] panel to make a useful clothes pin bag.

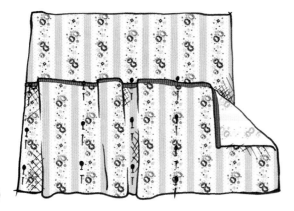

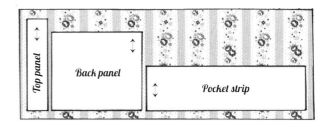

CUTTING OUT

Cut the pocket strip and back panel so that the pattern lies symmetrically.

- One 28$^1/_2$" x 8" [74 x 20 cm] pocket strip
- One 16$^1/_2$" x 14$^1/_4$" [42 x 36 cm] back panel
- One 16$^1/_2$" x 4" [42 x 10 cm] top panel

TO MAKE THE ORGANIZER

MARK THE POCKET DIVISIONS

Finish the top edge of the pocket strip with bias binding (see page 17). Using a fading marker pen and a ruler, draw three vertical lines across the pocket strip, one at the center and one 7$^1/_2$" [19 cm] in from each side edge. Fold the back panel in half widthwise and mark the center bottom edge with a pin. Add two more pins along the bottom edge, each 4$^1/_2$" [11 cm] in from the side edges. Then mark these same positions 8" [20 cm] up from the bottom edge.

01 Lay the back panel right-side up and place the pocket strip, right-side up, across the lower part. Pin the two together, matching the ends of the drawn lines and the pin positions. Add more pins along the pocket divisions, then pin the side edges together.

tip... THE TIDY IS DESIGNED AROUND A 13"-WIDE [33 CM-WIDE] WOODEN COAT HANGER. IF YOURS IS LARGER THAN THIS, YOU CAN EXTEND THE WIDTH AND POCKETS ACCORDINGLY.

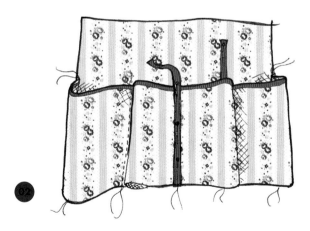

STITCH THE POCKETS

Baste the pocket strip to the back panel along the three dividing lines. Machine stitch, following the drawn lines. Sew the side edges together, taking a $3/8$" [1 cm] seam allowance.

02 Cut three $11^3/4$" [30 cm] lengths of bias binding. Pin and baste them centrally over the three dividing lines and then up along the panel—they end $2^1/2$" [6 cm] below the top edge. Machine stitch the binding in place with matching thread, sewing close to each edge. Sew every line of stitches in the same direction, from top to bottom, to prevent puckering.

FOLD THE PLEATS

03 Fold a $3/4$" [2 cm] double pleat at each corner of each pocket, pinning them so that they overlap the binding, but line up the two outside pleats just inside the stitching lines. Baste the folds down securely through all the layers. Machine stitch all along the bottom edge, stitching $1/4$" [6 mm] from the edge.

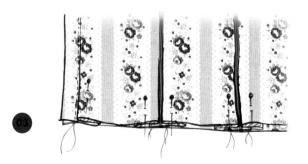

ADD THE TOP PANEL

04 Bind the bottom edge of the top panel, as before. Then lay it right-side up and place the coat hanger centrally on top, so that it lies $1/4$" [6 mm] below the top edge. Draw along the curve with a fading fabric marker pen, extending the line out to the side edges. Mark the position of the hook.

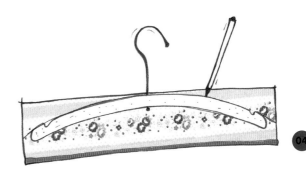

With the right side facing upward, pin and baste the top panel across the top edge of the back panel, matching the raw edges. Machine stitch the two together along the drawn line and the side edges, stitching $1/2$" [12 mm] from the side edges and leaving a $3/8$" [1 cm] opening at the marked point for the hook. Leave the bottom edge of the top panel open. Trim back the top edge $1/2$" [12 mm] from the stitching line.

ADD THE FINISHING TOUCHES

05 Using a large coin, draw a curve at each bottom corner and cut along the line. (This makes the corners easier to bind.)

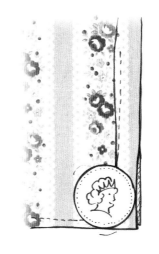

Sew the remaining binding all the way around the outside edge, starting and finishing at the center top edge and curving it around the corners (see page 17 for detailed binding instructions). Fold under a narrow turning at each end and leave $3/8$" [1 cm] unstitched on each side of the hook opening.

06 Slide the hanger under the top panel and ease the hook through the top opening. Push the hanger right up into place, so that it sits snugly inside the curve. Pin the bound straight edge of the top panel to the back panel and slip-stitch it in place along the edge of the binding. Sew the loose ends of the binding in place at the hook opening and stitch the folds together at the front and back. Make a small bow from the remaining binding and sew it to the base of the hook.

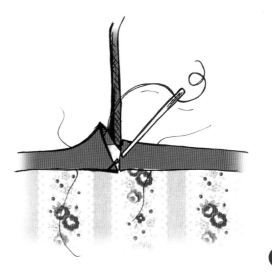

TAKE IT FURTHER

These pleated pockets are just the right size for shoes. You could easily extend the back panel and add another tier of pockets to make a useful holder to hang inside a closet or on the back of your bedroom door.

FOLD-UP TRAY

These versatile fabric trays—which can be made in any size—are quick and easy to run up, and make useful gifts. Put them all around the house as containers for cosmetics, letters, pencils and pens, a sewing kit, or loose change and keys.

MATERIALS & EQUIPMENT
TEMPLATE ON PAGES 156–157 (SEE BELOW)
24" x 12" [60 x 30 cm] of a medium-weight cotton print, for one tray
Matching sewing thread
5³/₄" [14.5 cm] square of strong cardboard
Sewing box (see page 8)
Sewing machine

SIZE
The template on pages 156 to 157 and the instructions are for the small tray pictured opposite, which has an approximately 8" [20 cm] square base and sides approximately 2" [5 cm] deep. To make the larger tray (visible in the background), which has an 10" [25 cm] square base and a 8" [20 cm] cardboard insert, adjust the template accordingly to increase the size, keeping the sides 2³/₁₆" [5.5 cm] deep.

CUTTING GUIDE
- Two panels the same size (cut using template)

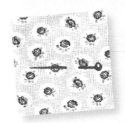

FABRIC CHOICE
I used the same fabric for both front and back panels, but try mixing a print and a polka dot, or a plain and patterned fabric to create different looks.

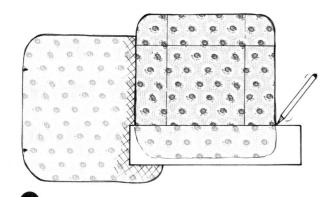

TO MAKE THE FOLD-UP TRAY

MARK THE STITCHING LINES
01 Following the template, mark the two A points on the wrong side of one panel. Lay the other panel right-side up on your work surface. Using a clear quilter's ruler and a fading fabric marker pen, draw a line 2³/₁₆" [5.5 cm] in from each edge.

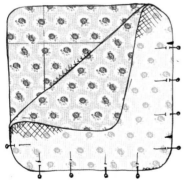

JOIN THE TWO PANELS

02 With right sides together and the panel with the marked A points on top, pin the two panels together, carefully matching up the curved corners. Baste, then machine stitch around the outside, taking a $^1/_4$" [6 mm] seam allowance and leaving the space between the two marked points open.

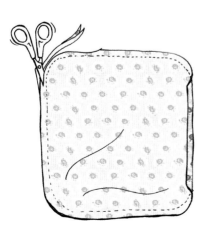

PRESS AND TRIM THE SEAM

03 Press the unstitched seam allowance inward on both sides, then trim the rest of the seam allowance down to $^1/_8$" [4 mm] all around. Turn right-side out, ease out the seams, and press lightly.

SEW ALONG THE STITCHING LINES

04 Baste the two layers together, just outside three of the marked stitching lines, leaving the line nearest the opening unstitched. Slide the square of cardboard through the opening, then baste just outside the fourth line. Using a zipper foot, machine stitch along the lines to hold the cardboard in place.

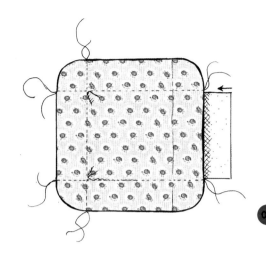

MACHINE STITCH THE OUTSIDE EDGE

05 Baste the two pressed seam allowances along the opening together to close the opening. Machine stitch all the way around, $1/8$" [4 mm] from the outside edge.

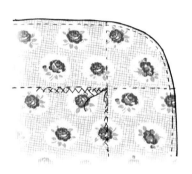

FORM THE CORNERS

06 Fold up the first corner so that the stitching lines meet at the top edge. Using a doubled length of thread, sew a few stitches at this point to hold the two sides together. Do the same at the other corners.

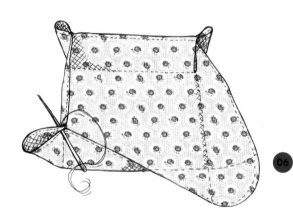

TAKE IT FURTHER

Making a template to your own size is very straightforward. Start by drawing the base on graph paper, then draw a line $2^3/16$" [5.5 cm] maway from each side. Round off the corners by drawing 2" [5 cm] diameter curves in each one, using a pencil and pair of compasses.

STORAGE CONTAINERS

I've always believed that everyday items don't need to be dull. These useful containers liven up any storage space, and will keep your work desk, sewing room, dressing table, or bathroom looking tidy at all times. If you are a beginner, you'll find that sewing the round base seam is a good lesson in basic sewing techniques.

MATERIALS & EQUIPMENT

TEMPLATE ON PAGE 155

FOR THE LARGE CONTAINER
32" x 12" [80 x 30 cm] each of a patterned (main) and plain (lining) medium-weight cotton fabric

FOR THE SMALL CONTAINER
26" x 10" [65 x 25 cm] each of plain (main) and patterned (lining) medium-weight cotton fabric

FOR BOTH CONTAINERS
4" x 2$\frac{1}{2}$" [10 x 6 cm] of medium-weight iron-on interfacing, for the label holder
A scrap of either the lining fabric or another contrasting fabric, for the label holder
2$\frac{3}{4}$" x 1$\frac{3}{8}$" [7 x 3.5 cm] rectangle of flexible clear plastic, for the label window
Double-sided tape
Matching sewing thread
Sewing box (see page 8)
Sewing machine

SIZE

LARGE: 6$\frac{1}{4}$" in diameter x 7$\frac{1}{4}$" tall [16 x 17 cm], with cuff folded down
SMALL: 5$\frac{1}{4}$" in diameter x 5$\frac{3}{4}$" tall [13 x 14 cm], with cuff folded down

CUTTING OUT

FROM THE MAIN FABRIC
• One base circle, 7" [18 cm] in diameter for large container OR 6" [15 cm] in diameter for small container
FROM LINING FABRIC
• One side panel, 20$\frac{1}{2}$" x 10" [52 x 25 cm] for large container OR 17" x 8" [43 x 20 cm] for small container

TO MAKE THE CONTAINERS

MAKE THE LABEL HOLDER
Following diagrams 01, 02, and 03 on pages 116 to 117, make the window-frame label holder with the interfacing piece and a scrap of either the lining fabric or another contrasting fabric. (See tip on page 53 for an alternative label holder.)

FABRIC CHOICE
You will need to use two fabrics that have a lot of body, such as furnishing fabrics, so that the boxes stand up by themselves; I combined calico with one of my classic little florals. Mix plains and prints, using up remnants and scraps from other projects.

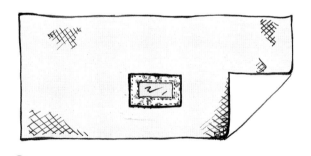

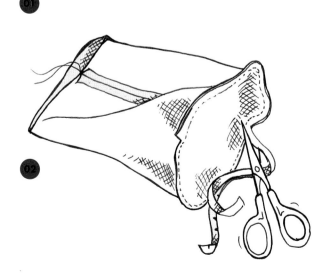

PREPARE THE SIDE PANEL

01 Pin the label holder centrally to the right side of the main fabric side panel, 3" [8 cm] up from the bottom edge on the large version or 2^1/$_2$" [6 cm] up for the small. Machine stitch along the side and bottom edges, sewing over the existing topstitching and leaving the top edge open.

With right sides together, pin and baste the side edges of the panel together. Machine stitch, taking a ^{3}/$_8$" [1 cm] seam allowance. Press the seam open.

ADD THE BASE

02 With right sides together and taking a ^{3}/$_8$" [1 cm] seam allowance, sew the main fabric base to the cylinder side panel (see page 15). Then carefully trim both layers of the seam allowance to ^{1}/$_4$" [6 mm]; this will give you a sharp angle at the base.

SEW THE LINING

03 With right sides together, pin the side edges of the lining panel together. Machine stitch, taking a ³/₈" [1 cm] seam allowance, leaving a 4" [10 cm] opening, ³/₄" [2 cm] up from the bottom end of the seam. Press the seam open, including the unstitched allowance.

Sew on the base in the same way as for the main piece, trim the seam allowance to ¹/₄" [6 mm], and turn right-side out.

PUT IT ALL TOGETHER

04 With right sides together, slip the lining inside the main piece, matching up the seams. Pin and baste the two together all the way around the top edge. Then machine stitch, taking a ³/₈" [1 cm] seam allowance.

05 Turn the whole thing right-side out through the opening in the lining seam, then slip-stitch the opening closed. Push the lining right down into the main part of the container and ease out the top seam. Press the top edge lightly. Then fold over the top edge to the outside to form a 2" [5 cm] cuff at the top of the large size or a 1¹/₂" [4 cm] cuff on the small size.

TAKE IT FURTHER

With the right fabric, this project could be enlarged to make a practical toy box or laundry container that can be folded up and put away when not in use.

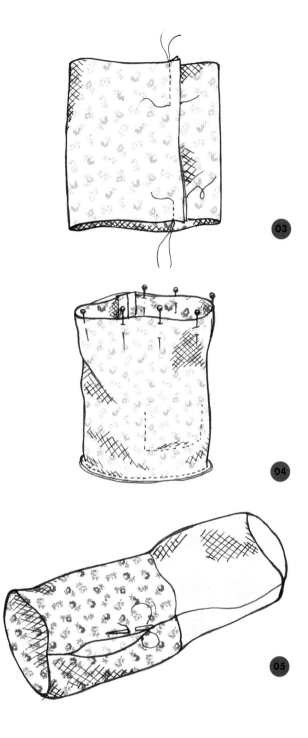

tip... A QUICK ALTERNATIVE TO THE FABRIC LABEL HOLDER IS TO CUT THE WINDOW SHAPE FROM A NON-FRAY FABRIC: THE LARGER BOX HAS A HOLDER MADE FROM RED FELT TO MATCH THE FLOWERS.

SEWING MACHINE COVER

Back in the 1880s, the first domestic sewing machines were thought of as part of the furniture and came complete with decoratively carved wooden boxes. Some machines still have their own hard cases, which are great for long-term storage. But half the time, when your machine is out on the table and in use, it's so much more practical to throw on this soft cover. And what's more, it looks great!

MATERIALS & EQUIPMENT

TEMPLATES ON PAGES 156–157

42" x 36" [100 x 80 cm] of a medium-weight cotton print
Matching sewing thread
Sewing box (see page 8)
Sewing machine

SIZE

It's a good idea to double check all the measurements against your sewing machine first, before cutting out the fabric. The cover is designed to fit over a standard domestic model with a carrying handle that lies toward the back of the arm. The handle opening is $5^1/2$" [14 cm] long. If your machine has a central handle, cut two $3^3/4$" x $6^1/4$" [9.5 x 16 cm] top panels instead. If the handle is longer than 5" [12 cm], lengthen the top pieces and reduce the top end of the side panels accordingly.

FABRIC CHOICE
All-over floral prints are ideal for simple, blocky projects like this Sewing Machine Cover and the pillows, which have large rectangular panels to show them off well.

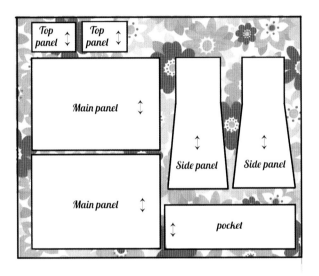

CUTTING OUT

- Two $16^1/2$" x $11^3/4$" [42 x 30 cm] main panels
- One $16^1/2$" x $6^1/4$" [42 x 16 cm] pocket
- Two side panels (cut using template)
- One $6^1/4$" x $3^1/8$" [16 x 8 cm] top panel
- One $6^1/4$" x $4^1/2$" [18 x 11 cm] top piece

TO MAKE THE COVER

SEW ON THE POCKET

01 Sew a double $3/8$" [1 cm] hem along the top edge of the pocket. Using a fading fabric marker pen and a ruler, draw a vertical line $5^1/8$" [13 cm] from the left edge. With both pieces right-side up, pin and baste the pocket to the bottom long edge of one main panel. Stitch together, $1/4$" [6 mm] from the side and bottom edges. Then sew along the drawn line, backstitching at the top end of the pocket.

MAKE IT SIMPLER

If you want to streamline the cover, cut the top panel from a single piece of fabric and omit the space for the handle.

PREPARE THE SIDE AND TOP PANELS

Press under ⅜" [1 cm] along the top edge of each of the two side panels. Stitch a double ⅜" [1 cm] hem along one long edge of each top panel and mark the center point of the other long edge.

CONSTRUCT THE HANDLE OPENING

02 With right sides together, position the two top panels along the folded-under edge of one of the side panels, with the hemmed edges facing the center. Position the short edges of the top panels ³⁄₁₆" [5 mm] in from the fold. Pin and baste them in place, then machine stitch, taking a ⅜" [1 cm] seam allowance.

03 Press the seam allowances toward the side panel. Machine topstitch ¼" [6 mm] from the edge of the side panel. Join the other side panel to the other edge of the top panels in the same way.

ADD THE MAIN PANELS

04 Fold the main panels in half and mark the center of the top edges. With right sides together, pin one main panel along one long edge of the joined pieces, matching the center to the center of the handle piece. Baste together, then machine stitch, taking a ⅜" [1 cm] seam allowance. Leave ⅜" [1 cm] unstitched at each end of the seam, reinforcing each end of the seam with a few backstitches.

05 Make a ¼" [6 mm] snip into the seam allowances of each side panel, directly below the seam ends. Align each side edge of the main panel with the edge of the adjacent side panel. Pin and baste together. With the side panel uppermost, stitch each seam from the top corner to the hem, taking a ⅜" [1 cm] seam allowance. Stitch the other main panel to the other side of the top and side panels in the same way.

Finish all the raw edges with an overlocking or zigzag stitch and press the seam allowances toward the side panels.

HEM THE BOTTOM EDGE

Trim the bottom edge as necessary, so that it is even all around, then finish it off with a double ⅜" [1 cm] hem.

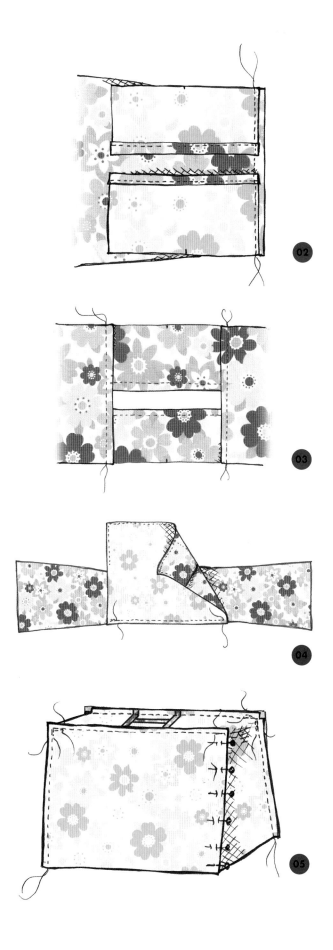

SEWING TIDY

This organizer may be the simplest project in the book, but it's bound to prove one of the most useful. The back section sits under your machine to protect the table top and the three front pockets keep your sewing tools conveniently close at hand. It's the companion piece to the Machine Cover, so choose fabrics with coordinating designs. Here, the grid pattern on the patchwork print simplifies cutting out the panels and stitching the pocket divisions.

MATERIALS & EQUIPMENT

22" x 38" [55 x 95 cm] of a medium-weight cotton print, for the main fabric
22" x 30" [55 x 75 cm] of a contrasting medium-weight cotton print, for the back panels
Matching sewing thread
Sewing box (see page 8)
Sewing machine

SIZE

19³/₄" x 27¹/₂" [50 x 70 cm]

CUTTING OUT

FROM MAIN FABRIC
- One 20¹/₂" x 28¹/₄" [52 x 72 cm] front panel
- One 20¹/₂" x 7" [52 x 17 cm] pocket

FROM CONTRASTING FABRIC
- One 20¹/₂" x 28¹/₄" [52 x 72 cm] back panel

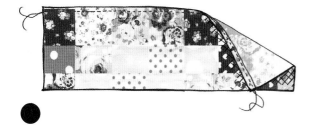

TO MAKE THE TIDY

PREPARE THE POCKET

01 Press under a ³/₈" [1 cm] turning along the top edge of the pocket and machine stitch, ¹/₄" [6 mm] from the fold.

ASSEMBLE THE FRONT

02 Position the pocket along the bottom edge of the front panel, with both pieces right-side up. Pin and baste the side and bottom edges of the pocket to the front panel.

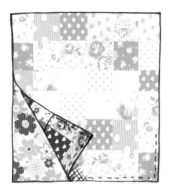

03

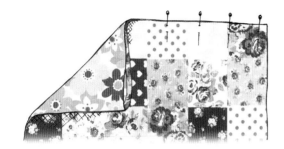

04

05

JOIN ON THE BACK PANEL

03 With right sides together, place the front panel over the back panel so that the pocket is sandwiched between them. Pin together along the side and bottom edges, leaving the top edge open. Machine stitch, taking a $3/8$" [1 cm] seam allowance, then clip the corners (see page 15). Press the seams inward, then press $3/8$" [1 cm] to the wrong side around the top edge. Turn right-side out and ease out the seams and corners. Press lightly.

04 Pin the front and back top edges together, then machine stitch, taking a $1/4$" [6 mm] seam allowance.

DIVIDE THE POCKET

05 Using a fading fabric marker pen, draw two vertical lines on the pocket, one halfway along, and the other 4" [10 cm] from the left edge. If your fabric has a distinct grid or striped pattern, like mine, adjust these measurements so that you can stitch along the nearest printed line. Pin the three layers together along the drawn lines and machine stitch along the lines. Reinforce the top end of each seam (i.e., the top end of the dividing line) with a few backstitches, so the pockets will stand up to wear.

tip... IF YOU WANT TO ADD AN EXTRA CUSHIONED LAYER TO THE TIDY, SIMPLY SLIP A RECTANGLE OF QUILT BATTING BETWEEN THE FRONT AND BACK BEFORE YOU SEW UP THE TOP EDGE.

TAKE IT FURTHER
Complete your sewing machine accessory set by making a 8" x 10" [20 x 25 cm] drawstring bag to store the pedal and cables. Follow the method used for the kids' Sport Bag (page 138), omitting the side loops and shortening the cords.

Easy

TORTOISE PINCUSHION

Every stitcher needs somewhere to store dressmaker's pins, so this tortoise is the ideal sewing companion. The shell is made using the English paper-patchwork technique, in which fabric-covered paper templates are hand-stitched together to form a mosaic pattern.

MATERIALS & EQUIPMENT

TEMPLATES ON PAGE 157

4" [10 cm] square each of six different lightweight cotton prints, for the shell

12" x 8" [30 x 20 cm] of a medium-weight cotton polka dot, for the base

Matching sewing thread

Polyester toy filling

Two black glass-headed pins or small black beads

Sewing box (see page 8)

Sewing machine

SIZE

Approximately 5" x 3¼" [12 x 8 cm]

CUTTING OUT

FROM PAPER
- One pentagon shell top
- Five shell sides
- One head
- One leg
- One tail

FROM POLKA DOT FABRIC
- Two bases

FABRIC CHOICE

Patchwork is a great way to practice some basic hand stitching, so use lightweight cotton fabrics that are easy to sew. I found six vintage dress fabrics for the shell, all with similarly small-scale patterns.

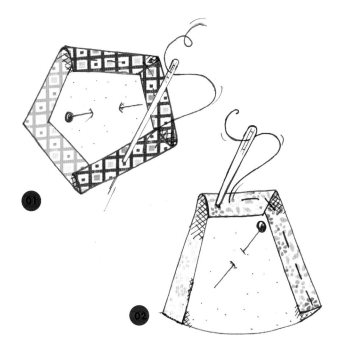

TO MAKE THE PINCUSHION

PREPARE THE PATCHES

01 Start with the pentagon at the center of the top of the shell. Pin the paper template to the wrong side of the first fabric and cut out, cutting about ³⁄₈" [1 cm] beyond the paper all around. Working with the wrong side facing you, fold over the seam allowance along each side in turn, basting it through the paper and fabric layers as you proceed.

02 Prepare the side and top edges of the five shell-side patches in the same way (using a different fabric for each one), but trim the fabric at the curved bottom edge level with the paper.

TAKE IT FURTHER

This is a practical, working tortoise, which is bound to appeal to children as well as stitchers. You could easily enlarge the pattern to make a larger toy version, but be sure to sew all of the seams securely, stuff it with safety-standard toy filling, and embroider the eyes with black thread. (Suitable for anybody aged over 36 months!)

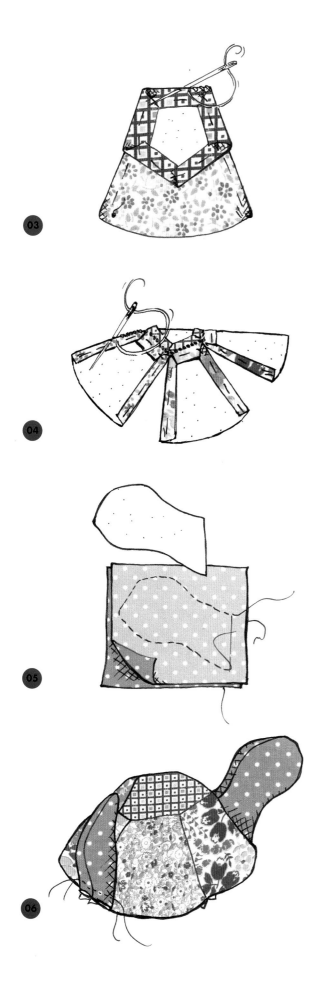

SEW THE SHELL TOGETHER

03 Place the pentagon along the top edge of a shell patch so that the corners match exactly. Starting at the right-hand corner, hand sew them together with tiny diagonal stitches, inserting the needle through both folded edges. Add the other four shell patches to the other four sides of the pentagon.

04 Now you have to join the adjacent straight edges of the shell patches. Fold the pentagon in half so that the two edges lie next to each other and hand sew as before. Repeat with the remaining straight shell patch edges, and make sure that you finish off each seam securely. Remove the basting threads and the papers. Turn right-side out.

ADD THE HEAD AND TAIL

05 Cut two pieces of polka dot fabric, about 4" x 3" [10 x 7.5 cm]. Using a fading fabric marker, draw around the head template on the wrong side of one piece. Pin the two pieces right sides together. Machine stitch around the head outline, leaving the neck edge open.

06 Cut out the head $3/16$" [3 mm] from the outline. Turn right-side out and stuff with toy filling, leaving the top $3/8$" [1 cm] unfilled. Fold the neck edge so that the two seam lines meet at the center and baste together. With right sides together, pin the neck edge centrally to the bottom edge of one shell patch. Machine stitch, taking a $1/4$" [6 mm] seam allowance.

Make and stuff the tail in the same way as the head, leaving the straight edge open. Fold the opening so that the two seams meet in the center, then baste it to the opposite side of the shell so that it lies across the seam between two shell patches. Machine stitch $1/4$" [6 mm] from the edge.

ADD THE LEGS

Make and stuff four legs in the same way as the head, leaving the top edges open. Sew them to the edge of the shell, positioning the front two so that they lie $3/8$" [1 cm] from each side of the head and the back two $3/8$" [1 cm] from the tail. Turn the shell the other way out so that the head, tail, and legs are lying inside it.

JOIN ON THE BASE

07 Pin the two base pieces together along the straight edge, with right sides together. Taking a $3/8$" [1 cm] allowance, machine stitch a short $5/8$" [1.5 cm] seam at each end, leaving an opening at the center. Press the seam open.

With right sides together, pin the base to the shell, matching the seam line to the seams in the head and tail. Ease the edges so that they fit together neatly: you may need to make a few tiny snips into the top of the legs, neck and tail so that the seam allowances curve around the base.

Baste securely. Machine stitch slowly and carefully around the edge, with the shell upward. Turn right-side out through the opening and stuff firmly. Slip-stitch the opening closed (see page 19).

Hand stitch the back of the neck to the shell about $3/8$" [1 cm] up from the seam, so that the head will face forward.

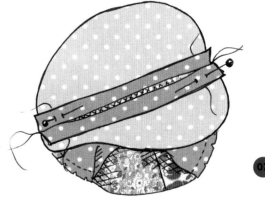

07

tip... AN ERASER-TIPPED PENCIL IS ALWAYS USEFUL FOR PUSHING IN THE POLYESTER FILLING WHEN YOU ARE STUFFING SMALL ITEMS, SUCH AS THE TORTOISE'S HEAD AND TAIL.

TRAVEL

ZIP-UP POUCHES

Here are two useful holiday accessories—a pair of space-saving, zip-up pouches that will hold all your essentials, whether travel documents or laundry. They are super quick to create from a single rectangle of fabric, and a good way to practice sewing in a zipper. Both bags are made in exactly the same way.

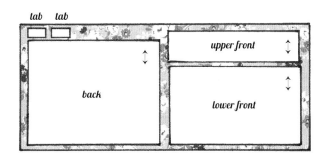

MATERIALS & EQUIPMENT

FOR THE LARGE POUCH

38" x 20" [95 x 50 cm] of a medium-weight cotton print
16" [40 cm] zipper, 1$\frac{1}{4}$" [3 cm] wide

FOR THE SMALL POUCH

28" x 14" [70 x 35 cm] of a medium-weight cotton print
12" [30 cm] zipper, 1$\frac{1}{4}$" [3 cm] wide

FOR BOTH POUCHES

8" [20 cm] of ribbon or cotton tape, $\frac{3}{8}$" [1 cm] wide
Matching sewing thread
Sewing box (see page 8)
Sewing machine

SIZE

LARGE: 16$\frac{1}{2}$" x 12$\frac{1}{2}$" [42 x 32 cm]
SMALL: 12$\frac{1}{2}$" x 8$\frac{1}{4}$" [32 x 21 cm]

CUTTING OUT

FOR THE LARGE POUCH

- One 17$\frac{1}{4}$" x 10$\frac{1}{4}$" [45 x 26 cm] lower front
- One 17$\frac{1}{4}$" x 4" [45 x 10 cm] upper front
- One 17$\frac{1}{4}$" x 13$\frac{1}{4}$" [45 x 35 cm] back

FOR THE SMALL POUCH

- One 13$\frac{1}{4}$" x 7" [35 x 17 cm] lower front
- One 13$\frac{1}{4}$" x 2$\frac{1}{2}$" [35 x 6 cm] upper front
- One 13$\frac{1}{4}$" x 9" [35 x 23 cm] back

FOR BOTH POUCHES

- Two end tabs, 2$\frac{1}{2}$" x 1$\frac{1}{4}$" [6 x 3 cm]

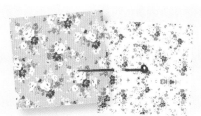

FABRIC CHOICE

Simple projects like this can easily be made from remnants that you have at hand. A variety of prints and fabrics will work, but make sure you use a medium-weight fabric so that the bags hold their shape. Make it fresh and modern with bright, contrasting zippers.

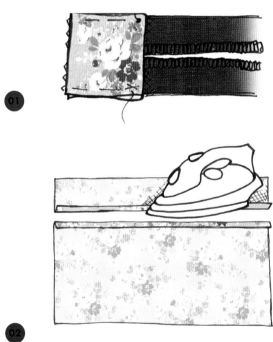

TO MAKE THE ZIP-UP POUCH

PREPARE THE ZIPPER

Fold and press the two end tabs in half widthwise, with the right side of the fabric facing outward.

01 Place one tab across each end of the zipper, so that the folded edges face inward. The distance between the raw outside edges should be the same as the width of the bag pieces—either 17^1/$_4$" [45 cm] or 13^1/$_4$" [35 cm]. Adjust the positions as necessary, then baste the top and bottom edges of the tabs to the zipper tapes.

SEW THE POUCH PIECES TOGETHER

02 Press ^{3}/$_8$" [6 mm] to the wrong side along the top edge of the lower front and the bottom edge of the upper front.

03 With the right side facing upward, baste the folded edge of the lower front along the bottom zipper tape, ^{1}/$_4$" [6 mm] from the center of the teeth. Using a zipper, machine stitch the two together ^{1}/$_8$" [4 mm] from the fold.

Baste and machine stitch the upper front to the top zipper tape in the same way. Open the zipper.

04 With right sides together, pin the back panel to the completed front and baste the two together all the way around the outside edge. Machine stitch, taking a 3/8" [1 cm] seam allowance, then finish the raw edges with an overlocking or zigzag stitch.

05 Clip the corners (see page 15) and turn the bag right-side out through the open zipper. Ease out the corners and press lightly. As a finishing touch, thread the ribbon or cotton tape through the zipper pull, knot it, and trim the ends at an angle.

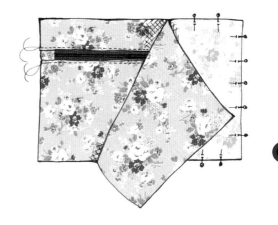

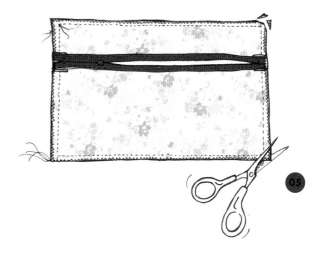

TAKE IT FURTHER

Add further pops of color to the pouches by using a bright, plain medium-weight fabric for the back of the pouch and a different bright, plain color for the front tabs.

GLASSES CASE

This classic glasses case is a really quick make, sewn together with just a few straight seams. What makes it special, however, is the spring clip fastener. This useful fastener is made up of two narrow strips of metal that slot into the top channel of the case, giving a well-finished look to the project.

MATERIALS & EQUIPMENT

16" x 4³/4" [40 x 12 cm] of a medium-weight cotton stripe, for the main-fabric piece for the outer case
13¹/4" x 5" [32 x 12 cm] of a lightweight cotton polka dot, for the lining piece
Matching sewing thread
3¹/2" [9 cm] spring clip
Sewing box (see page 8)
Sewing machine

SIZE

3¹/2" x 7" [9 x 17 cm]

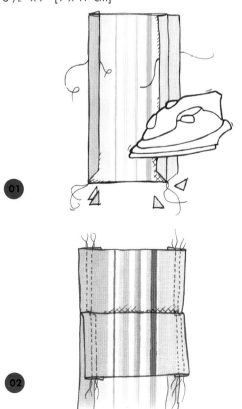

TO MAKE THE GLASSES CASE

PREPARE THE OUTER CASE

Fold the 16" x 4³/4" [40 x 12 cm] main-fabric piece in half widthwise, with right sides together. Pin and baste the side edges together, then mark a point 2" [5 cm] down from each top corner. Machine stitch the side edges between these two points, taking a ⁵/8" [1.5 cm] seam allowance and reinforcing each end of the seam (see page 14).

01 Clip off the bottom corners diagonally to within ¹/8" [4 mm] of the stitching to reduce the bulk. Press the seam allowances, including the unstitched top ends, inward.

02 Sew down each of the four unstitched seam allowances with two parallel rows of stitches. Start each double row at the top. Stitch ¹/4" [6 mm] from outside edge for 2" [5 cm], then work two stitches at a right angle, turn fabric round again and stitch back to the top edge, ¹/8" [4 mm] from first line of stitching.

tip... FOR A FUN PERSONALIZED TOUCH, WHY NOT USE CHAIN STITCH TO CREATE A MONOGRAM OF YOUR INITIALS (OR EMBROIDER ON YOUR TELEPHONE NUMBER, SO YOU NEVER LOSE IT!). TURN TO PAGE 18, TO SEE HOW TO WORK ALL THE HAND STITCHES.

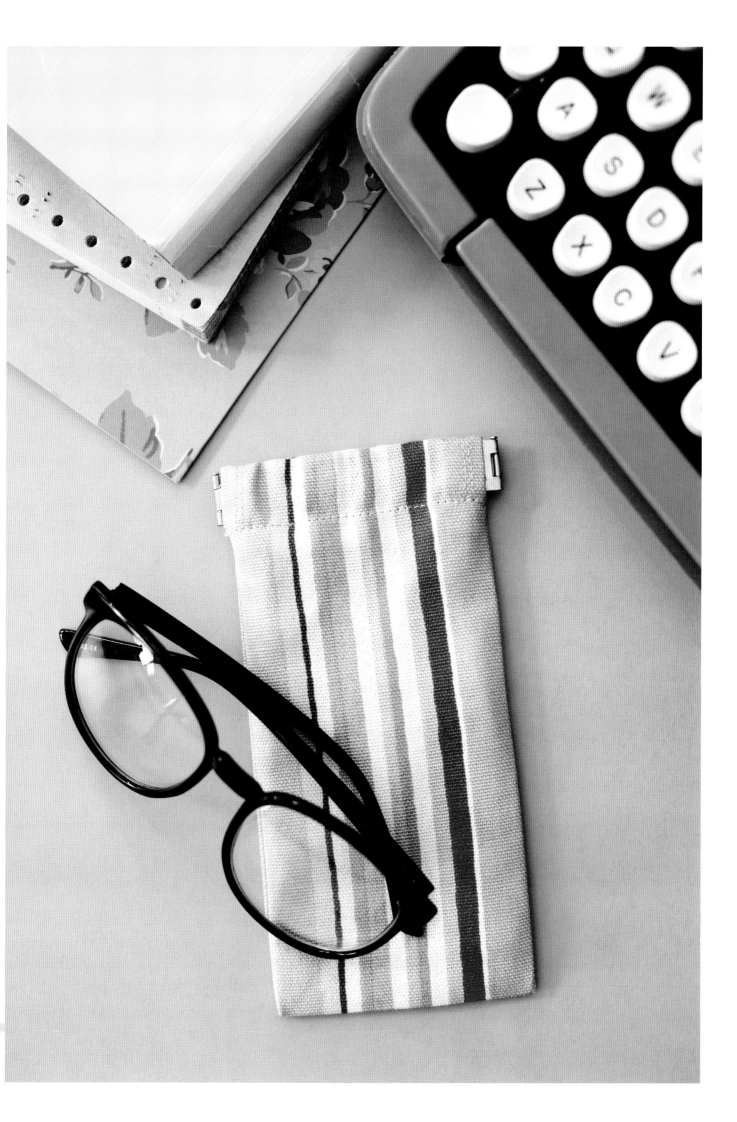

tip... IF YOU ARE USING A FABRIC THAT HAS A DISTINCTIVE LINEAR MOTIF RUNNING THROUGH IT, WHETHER IT'S A STRIPE LIKE THIS OR A BAND OF PRINTED FLOWERS, YOU SHOULD ALWAYS ALLOW A LITTLE EXTRA WIDTH SO THAT YOU CAN CENTER THE DESIGN.

03 Press under and then baste down a 1" [2.5 cm] hem along each top edge to make the spring-clip channels. With the right side facing upward, machine stitch down the raw edges, $3/4$" [2 cm] from the fold. Work a few backstitches over the two seam lines to strengthen the join. Turn the case right-side out, ease out the corners and press lightly.

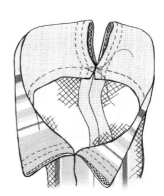

SEW THE LINING

04 Fold the $12^1/_2$" x $4^3/_4$" [32 x 12 cm] lining in half widthwise with right sides together and join the side edges, taking a $5/_8$" [1.5 cm] seam allowance. Clip the corners, then press the seams inward, as for the outer case. Press $3/_8$" [1 cm] to the wrong side around the top edge.

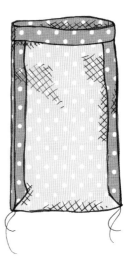

PUT IT ALL TOGETHER

05 Slip the lining right inside the outer case, aligning the side seams. Push it right down so that the folded top edge is aligned with the stitching line around the top of the outer case. Baste the two together, then hand sew together with slip-stitches.

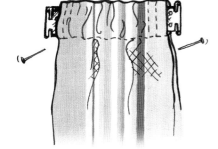

06 Slide one half of the spring clip into each channel and, following the manufacturer's instructions, join them together with the pins provided.

TAKE IT FURTHER

Spring clips, also known as flex frames, are available in widths up to 5" [12.5 cm], so you could adapt this project to make a purse or a phone case.

POCKET SEWING KIT

This fold-up purse is based on a traditional sewing organizer, with pockets for all the essentials—needles, pins, threads, and embroidery scissors. Slim and versatile, you could also use it to hold your travel tickets and small change, or to keep precious jewels safe, tucked away in a suitcase.

MATERIALS & EQUIPMENT

TEMPLATES ON PAGE 156

20" x 20" [50 x 50 cm] of a lightweight cotton print

4³/₄" [5 cm] zipper

1¹/₂ yards [130 cm] of bias binding, ¹/₂" [12 mm] wide

Sewing thread to match the fabric and the bias binding

Two small buttons

Sewing box (see page 8)

Sewing machine

SIZE

5¹/₂" x 3¹/₄" [14 x 8 cm], when folded

FABRIC CHOICE

A cute, small print is ideal for this kind of intricate project. For this purse, which stars on the front cover of the book, I used my classic Little Bird print in a bright, new colorway.

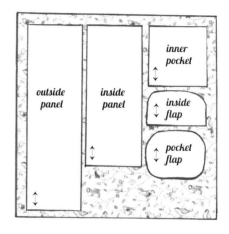

CUTTING OUT

- One inside flap (cut using template)
- One pocket flap (cut using template)
- One 5¹/₂" x 14¹/₄" [14 x 36 cm] inside panel
- One 5¹/₂" x 17³/₄" [14 x 45 cm] outside panel
- One 5¹/₂" x 6" [14 x 15 cm] inner pocket

TO MAKE THE SEWING KIT

PREPARE THE OUTSIDE PANEL

01 Pin the inside flap template to the bottom end of the outside panel, cut around the curved edges, and remove the template.

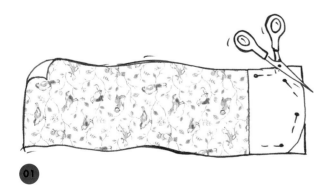

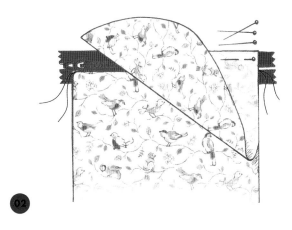

INSERT THE ZIPPER

Place the inside panel right-side up on your work surface. Position the zipper centrally along the top edge, with the right side facing downward and the pull at the left-hand edge. Pin and then baste the top half of the zipper to the fabric.

02 Fold the zipper over so that the right side is facing upward. Lay the inside flap right-side down along the other edge of the zipper tape. Check that the side edges of the flap line up exactly with those of the inside panel, then pin and baste the top edge to the zipper. Using thread to match the fabric, sew the zipper in place and then topstitch $1/8$" [4 mm] from the teeth.

JOIN THE OUTSIDE AND INSIDE PANELS

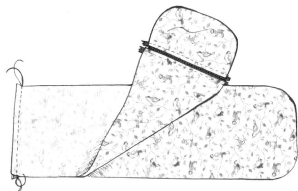

03 With right sides together, pin the inside and outside panels together along the straight bottom edge. Pin, baste, and machine stitch, taking a $1/4$" [6 mm] seam allowance. Refold so that the fabric is right side out. Line up and pin together the two curved edges, then pin along the long side edges. Baste all the way around and press the bottom edge. The bottom-edge seam will now be on the inside.

MAKE THE POCKETS

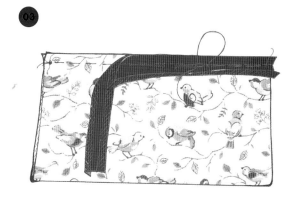

Mark a point on each side of the inside panel, $3^{1}/8$" [8 cm] up from the straight bottom edge. Fold up the fabric between these points to make the lower pocket. Pin and baste the side edges together and press.

04 Fold the inner pocket in half lengthwise, with the right side facing outward. Pin and baste the two long edges together and press. Finish the basted edge with a 6" [15 cm] length of bias binding (see page 17).

05 Pin the inner pocket in place $^5/_8$" [1.5 cm] above the lower pocket and baste down the side and bottom edges. Machine stitch the bottom edge of the inner pocket close to the fold.

06 Using a fading fabric marker pen, draw a line $^3/_8$" [1 cm] above the inner pocket and a second line $^3/_8$" [1 cm] above the zipper. Machine stitch across these two lines.

BIND THE OUTER EDGE

Trim the ends of the zipper tape in line with the side edges. Then finish the side and curved edges with bias binding.

MAKE THE POCKET FLAP

07 Fold the pocket flap in half lengthwise, with the right side facing outward. Line up the curved edges carefully, then pin and baste them together. Bind the raw edges with the remaining bias binding, turning under $^3/_8$" [1 cm] at each end.

Pin the straight edge of the flap $^1/_4$" [4 mm] above the inner pocket. Baste it in place, then machine close to the fold. Turn the flap back over to the right side and press along the seam.

ADD THE FINISHING TOUCHES

08 Using two strands of sewing thread to match the binding, make a $^1/_2$" [12 mm] buttonhole loop in the center of both flaps, as shown on page 20. Sew one of the buttons to the inner pocket, in line with the buttonhole loop on the pocket flap. Turn up the bottom edge twice, then fold over the top flap. Sew the second button to the outside, in line with the top flap buttonhole loop.

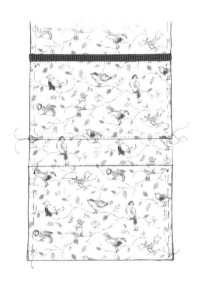

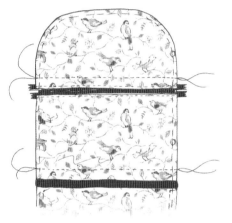

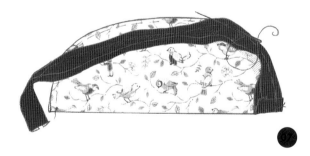

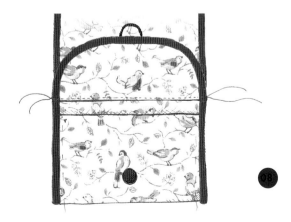

EYE MASK

This lightly quilted eye mask is lined with striped cotton and comes complete with its own matching drawstring pouch. The mask is edged with striped bias binding, so this project is a good way to learn about binding both inside and outside curves (see page 17). The strap elastic is inside a narrow fabric tube. The handy technique for sewing narrow tubes, known as rouleaux, can be used for all kinds of ties, straps, and loops.

MATERIALS & EQUIPMENT

TEMPLATES ON PAGES 154–155

22" x 10" [55 x 25 cm] of a lightweight floral cotton, for the mask and pouch

9" x 6" [22 x 12 cm] of a lightweight plain cotton, for the mask backing

22" x 14" [55 x 35 cm] of a brushed cotton stripe, for the lining

9" x 4" [22 x 12 cm] of a plain cotton, for the tassels (optional)

$1^1/4$ yards [1 m] of striped bias binding, $^3/4$" [2 cm] wide (plus an optional $^3/4$ yard [35 cm] extra, for tassels)

10" x 6" [22 x 12 cm] of cotton or bamboo quilt batting

12" [30 cm] of elastic, $^3/16$" [5 mm] wide

16" [40 cm] of filler cord, $^1/8$" [3 mm] in diameter

12" [30 cm] of silky cord, $^1/8$" [3 mm] in diameter, for the drawstrings

Matching sewing thread

Six-strand embroidery floss in cream

Small safety pin

Sewing box (see page 8)

Sewing machine

SIZE

POUCH: $5^1/4$" x $6^1/4$" [13 x 16 cm]
EYE MASK: 8" x $3^1/2$" [20 x 9 cm]

CUTTING OUT

FROM FLORAL FABRIC
- One 9" x 5" [22 x 12 cm] rectangle, for the eye mask
- Two $5^1/2$" x 8" [14 x 20 cm] rectangles for the pouch

FROM BRUSHED-COTTON STRIPED FABRIC
- One eye mask (cut using template)
- One 20" x $1^1/2$" [50 x 4 cm] strip, for the eye mask strap
- Two $5^1/2$" x 8" [14 x 20 cm] rectangles, for the pouch lining

FROM PLAIN BACKING FABRIC
- One 9" x 5" [22 x 12 cm] rectangle, for the eye mask

FROM BATTING
- One 9" x 5" [22 x 12 cm] rectangle, for the eye mask

FROM PLAIN TASSEL FABRIC OR SEAMED BINDING
- Four $2^3/4$" [7 cm] tassel circles (cut using template)

FABRIC CHOICE

The brushed cotton we chose is ideal for the eye mask, as it feels wonderfully soft against your skin: cotton velvet or smooth satin would be good alternatives. You could even make this out of an old pair of flannel pajamas. Here we used a diagonal trim and striped tassels to give our design a nice energy.

TO MAKE THE EYE MASK

QUILT THE FABRIC

Pin the eye mask template to the right side of the floral rectangle and draw around the edge with a fading fabric marker pen. Using a clear ruler, mark a ¾" [2 cm] diamond grid across the surface as a guideline for the quilting. Place the plain cotton backing rectangle on your work surface. Lay the batting over it, then put the floral fabric right-side up on top. Pin them together, then baste through all three layers, ⅛" [4 mm] inside the eye-mask outline.

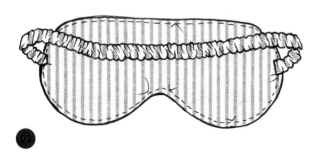

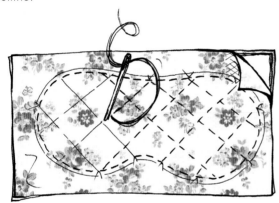

MAKE IT SIMPLER

The striped tassel ends are inspired by traditional Indian textiles. To make them, press the matching binding flat and join two 3¼" [8 cm] lengths with a narrow seam so that it is wide enough for cutting out the circles. Alternatively, make tassels from circles of a contrasting plain fabric—they will look equally good.

01 Stitch along each of the grid lines by hand, using three strands of cream embroidery floss. Be sure to start and finish each row at the basting line so that the ends of the thread won't unravel when the mask is cut out. When you have finished, cut carefully along the outline. With the right side facing outward, pin and baste the striped lining fabric eye-mask shape to the back. Machine stitch all four layers together, ⅛" [4 mm] from the edge. Insert pins at each side, at the points indicated on the template.

ADD THE STRAP

Fold the strap strip in half lengthwise, with the right sides together. Machine stitch all the way along the long raw edge, ¼" [6 mm] from the edge and turn right-side out (see how to do this on page 21).

02 Now attach the safety pin to one end of the elastic. Push it through the fabric tube and sew the two securely together at each end by hand. Fold back the raw edges and stitch the ends to the back of the mask, between the two points marked on the template.

BIND THE OUTER EDGE

Finish the outer edge with striped bias binding, starting the round at the center top edge (see page 17).

TO MAKE THE POUCH

PIPE THE BAG

Cut a 15" [38 cm] strip of bias binding. Open out the folds and press it flat, taking care not to stretch the fabric. Fold the strip centrally over the filler cord and baste it in place close to the cord. Trim the raw edges so the piping seam allowance is ⅝" [15 mm] wide.

03 Insert a pin 3½" [9 cm] down from the top corners on each side of a bag piece. With the raw edges matching and the right side of the fabric facing upward, pin and baste the piping around the edge of the bag, between the pins. You will need to make a little snip into the binding at each corner so that it will bend around neatly: cut to within $1/8$" [4 mm] of the cord. Taper the ends of the binding across the edge of the fabric just below the marker pins.

ADD THE LINING

04 With right sides together, pin and baste a lining piece to the top edge of each bag piece. Machine stitch, taking a $1/4$" [4 mm] seam allowance, then press the seams open. Pin and baste the two sides of the bag together, carefully matching up the seams. Machine stitch all around, stitching $3/8$" [1 cm] from the edge and curving the line around the piping, leaving an $3^1/4$" [8 cm] opening at the top edge and a $3/4$" [2 cm] opening just above the piping on each side (these short openings are for the gathering channel). Trim the surplus fabric from the corners and press the seam allowances inward, over the bag and lining. Turn the whole thing right-side out by pulling the main bag through the large opening. Ease out the seams and corners, then turn under the fabric along the large opening so that it's level with the stitching line. Pin the two sides of the opening together and sew by hand or machine.

05 Push the bag down into the lining, easing it right down into the corners. Baste the two layers together along the seam line, $1^1/2$" [4 cm] below the top edge. Make the gathering channel for the cords by working two lines of stitches around the bag, $1/2$" [1 cm] apart and aligned with the channel openings. Then turn the bag right-side out.

ADD THE DRAWSTRINGS AND TASSELS

Cut the silky cord in half. Fix a safety pin to one end and thread it all the way through the gathering channel, starting and ending at the right-hand opening. Thread the second cord through the left-hand opening in the same way.

06 Fold one of the tassel circles into quarters and carefully piece a hole at the center with the point of your embroidery scissors. Push the end of a cord through the hole, then knot the end. Thread a needle with cream embroidery floss and stitch the fabric to the cord. Bind the thread tightly around the top of the cord a few times, then fasten off securely. Add tassels to the other cords and roll up the circles to make them into tassel shapes.

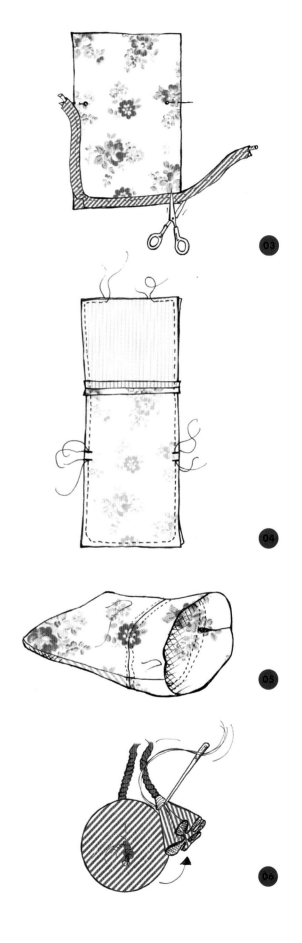

WASH BAG

Perfect for holidays, stylish enough for the bathroom shelf, this softly padded wash bag is surprisingly straightforward to put together. I love the T-junction seams at the bottom corners, which create a squared-off shape, making the bag roomy and ensuring it will stand up easily.

MATERIALS & EQUIPMENT

32" x 12" [80 x 30 cm] of a printed terry cloth
32" x 12" [80 x 30 cm] of single-sided fusible fleece, for the backing
32" x 12" [80 x 30 cm] of shower-curtain fabric, for the lining
12" [30 cm] zipper
6" [15 cm] of cotton tape, $^3/_8$" [1 cm] wide
Matching sewing thread
Sewing box (see page 8)
Sewing machine

FABRIC CHOICE

You could make this bag out of cotton, but I liked the quirky appeal of using this fifties terry-cloth print, which I picked up at the market. We used a water-resistant woven shower curtain fabric for the lining, which is easier to stitch than plasticized cloth.

SIZE

12" x 8" x 4" [30 x 20 x 10 cm]

CUTTING OUT

Cut the zipper ends from the terry cloth, then iron the rest of the fabric to the fusible fleece, following the manufacturer's instructions.

FROM TERRY CLOTH
● Two 1" x 1" [2.5 x 2.5 cm] zipper ends

FROM FLEECE-BACKED TERRY CLOTH
● Two 13$^3/_4$" x 10$^3/_4$" [35 x 27 cm] bag panels

FROM SHOWER-CURTAIN FABRIC
● Two 13$^3/_4$" x 10$^3/_4$" [35 x 27 cm] lining pieces

TO MAKE THE WASHBAG

PREPARE THE T-JUNCTION SEAMS

Cut a 2" [5 cm] square from the bottom corners of the two bag panels and the two lining pieces.

SEW ON THE ZIPPER

01 Do up the zipper. With right sides together, pin a small square zipper end across each end of the tapes. Stitch in place, taking a $^1/_4$" [6 mm] seam allowance. Press the squares outward and stitch across the terry cloth, just inside the seam line.

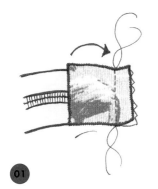
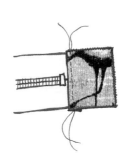

01

02 With right sides together, pin and baste one edge of the zipper along the top edge of one bag panel. Thread your machine with matching sewing thread and fit on the zipper foot. Stitch the zipper in place, stitching ¹/₄" [6 mm] from the teeth: remember to move the zipper puller as necessary (see page 20). Join the other side of the zipper to the second panel in the same way.

SEW THE BAG PANELS TOGETHER

03 Open up the zipper and fold the bag so that the right sides of the front and back panels are together and match up exactly. Baste the side and bottom edges together. Machine stitch the bottom edge, taking a ³/₈" [1 cm] seam allowance. Sew the two side edges, from the bottom corners toward the top. Refold the bottom corners and sew the T-junction seams (see page 15).

ADD THE LINING

04 Press under ¹/₄" [6 mm] along the top edge of each lining piece, then sew together the lining in the same way as the bag. Turn it right-side out and slide it over the bag, matching up the side seams. Pin and baste the pressed edge to the zipper tape ¹/₄" [6 mm] from the teeth and slip-stitch it in place. Turn the bag right-side out. Thread the tape through the zipper pull, stitch just below the hole and trim the ends at an angle.

LAPTOP CASE

Laptops are such a personal item, a custom-made case is a great way to reflect your own unique style. A bold fabric—like this textured vintage seersucker—will lift it out of the ordinary. You will need to adapt the size to the measurements of your own laptop, so this project is a good lesson in drafting patterns.

MATERIALS & EQUIPMENT

FOR A 13" [33 CM] LAPTOP

33" x 16" [80 x 40 cm] of a lightweight or medium-weight cotton print, for the main fabric

33" x 16" [80 x 40 cm] of a medium-weight polka dot cotton, for the lining

33" x 16" [80 x 40 cm] of cotton or bamboo quilt batting

24" [60 cm] zipper

2^3/$_4$ yards [2.5 m] of bias binding, ^{1}/$_2$" [12 mm] wide

FOR A 17" [43 CM] LAPTOP

39" x 20" [100 x 50 cm] of a lightweight or medium-weight cotton print, for the main fabric

39" x 20" [100 x 50 cm] of a medium-weight cotton polka dot, for the lining

39" x 20" [100 x 50 cm] of cotton or bamboo quilt batting

28" [70 cm] zipper

3^1/$_2$ yards [3 m] of bias binding, ^{1}/$_2$" [12 mm] wide

FOR BOTH SIZES

Matching sewing thread

Sewing pattern paper or quilter's graph paper

Sewing box (see page 8)

Sewing machine

SIZE

Use these measurements as a guide for a different-sized laptop, remembering it's better to have more fabric than less.

CUTTING OUT

Draw the panel templates as instructed on page 86.

FROM MAIN FABRIC

- Two rectangles, for the side panels—each one 1^1/$_4$" [3 cm] wider and 1^1/$_4$" [3 cm] deeper than the laptop
- One gusset panel

FROM BATTING

- Two side-panel rectangles, the same size as the main-fabric rectangles
- One gusset panel

FROM LINING FABRIC

- Two side-panel rectangles, the same size as the main-fabric rectangles
- One gusset panel
- One 6" x 2^1/$_2$" [15 x 6 cm] handle piece

FABRIC CHOICE

A contrasting lining works well here: my Laptop Case is lined with my Spot fabric in red, to give you an unexpected glimpse of bright color when the case is opened.

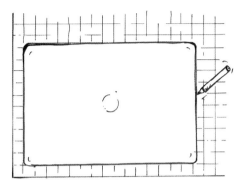

TO MAKE THE LAPTOP CASE

01 To make the side panel template, place your laptop on the graph paper, matching the edges up along the grid. Draw around the outside edge, then cut out along the printed lines, ignoring the curved corners.

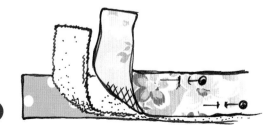

02 Using a pencil and a pair of compasses, draw a quarter circle with a radius of $1^{1}/4$" [3 cm] at each corner of the paper rectangle and cut along these lines.

Measure all around the edge of the template, then subtract the length of the zipper from this figure. Add on $1^{1}/4$" [3 cm], then cut a strip of paper this length and the same width as your zipper for the gusset template.

QUILT THE SIDE PANELS

Fold one main-fabric rectangle in half widthwise to find the center top and bottom. Using a fading fabric marker pen and a ruler, draw a line between these two points, then draw a series of parallel vertical lines outward, spacing them $2^{1}/4$" [6 cm] apart. Place a rectangle of lining fabric right-side down on your work surface, with batting on top and a main-fabric rectangle right-side up on top of the batting. Baste the three layers securely together, sewing a line of long stitches $1/4$" [6 mm] from each of the drawn lines. Machine stitch along each drawn line. Repeat with the remaining side panel pieces.

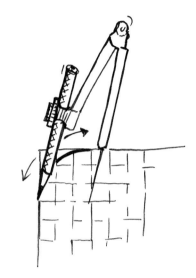

03 Pin the side panel template centrally to one finished panel and cut out. Finish the edge with a round of zigzag or overlocking stitch. Repeat with the second quilted side panel. Fold both panels in half widthwise and mark the center of the bottom edges with the fading fabric marker pen.

PREPARE THE GUSSET

04 Place the gusset lining strip right-side down on your work surface, with batting on top and the main-fabric gusset strip right-side up on top of the batting. Pin and baste them together, then zigzag or overlock sttich the edges. Fold in half widthwise and mark the center of each long edge with the fading fabric marker pen.

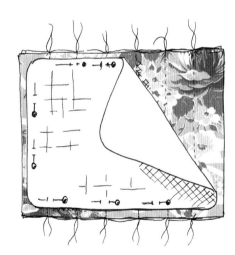

05 Close the zipper. With right sides together, pin the ends of the zipper tapes to the short ends of the gusset. Baste in place, $^5/_8$" [1.5 cm] from the edge. Place the resulting loop around one side panel to double check the fit and adjust the seams if necessary. Machine stitch along the basted lines, then trim the seam allowance to $^1/_4$" [6 mm]. Zigzag stitch and then bind the raw edges (see page 17). Baste the binding onto the gusset so that it lies flat.

PUT IT ALL TOGETHER

With right sides together, pin the center of the gusset to the center bottom edge of one side panel. Pin the gusset and the zipper tape all the way around the outside edge of the panel.

06 Baste the two pieces together, using lots of small stitches around the corners. Machine stitch, taking a $^1/_4$" [6 mm] seam allowance and sewing slowly and carefully.

07 Open up the zipper, then pin and baste the second side panel to the other side of the zipper tape in the same way. Machine stitch, sewing in the same direction to stop the gusset from puckering. Cover each seam allowance with bias binding, stretching the binding gently at the corners to get a smooth finish.

08 Turn the case right-side out and close the zipper. Using the lining-fabric handle piece, make the handle as shown on page 21 and place it centrally along the gusset on the same side as the zipper pull. Move each end in by $^3/_8$" [1 cm] to create a slight loop, then baste the ends to the case. Sew in place securely by hand or machine.

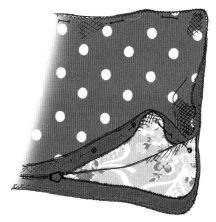

TAKE IT FURTHER

You can easily adapt this project to fit any size laptop. If you want to make a case for a tablet computer, however, you will need a narrower (1" [2.5 cm]) zipper. Cut the gusset to the same width.

BAGS

TOTE BAG

This practical tote has plenty of room for books or shopping, and the topstitched side edges give it a boxy, finished look. You'll see that this is the same basic shape as the Lunch Bag (page 132), so if you make one, you'll find the other project a cinch.

MATERIALS & EQUIPMENT

55" x 28" [140 x 70 cm] of a medium-weight cotton print, for the main fabric

39" x 24" [100 x 60 cm] of a medium-weight cotton polka dot, for the lining

Matching sewing thread

Sewing box (see page 8)

Sewing machine

SIZE

13" x 17$^{1}/_{4}$" x 3$^{1}/_{4}$"[33 x 44 x 8 cm], excluding handles

CUTTING OUT

FROM MAIN FABRIC

- Two 13$^{3}/_{4}$" x 20" [35 x 50 cm] bag panels
- Two 4" x 18" [10 x 46 cm] side panels
- Two 26" x 3$^{1}/_{4}$" [65 x 8 cm] handle strips
- One 8" x 6" [20 x 15 cm] pocket

FROM LINING FABRIC

- Two 13$^{3}/_{4}$" x 19" [35 x 48 cm] bag panels
- Two 4" x 17" [10 x 43 cm] side panels

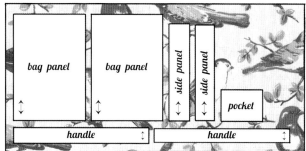

MAIN FABRIC

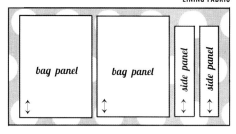

LINING FABRIC

TO MAKE THE TOTE BAG

JOIN THE MAIN BAG PANELS

With right sides together, pin the bottom edges of the two main-fabric bag panels together. Baste, then machine stitch, taking a $^{3}/_{8}$" [1 cm] seam allowance. Press the seam allowance to one side. Topstitch the seam (see page 15).

ADD THE SIDE PANELS

01 Use a fading fabric marker pen to mark the $^{3}/_{8}$" [1 cm] seam allowance along the bottom edge of the first main-fabric side panel. Mark the center 2" [5 cm] along) and the $^{3}/_{8}$" [1 cm] seam allowance at the side edges. With right sides together, line the center mark up with the base seam of the bag. Pin and baste in place. Stitch along the seam line, leaving the seam allowances unstitched. Reinforce both ends of the seam with backstitches.

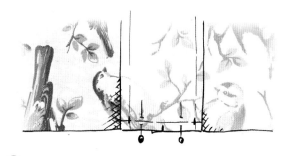

01

MAKE IT SIMPLER

The bag is double-layered so that it will stand up to a lot of everyday use, but you can easily omit the lining. Bind or overlock stitch the seams (see page 17) to finish the inside seams and finish off the top edge with a double hem.

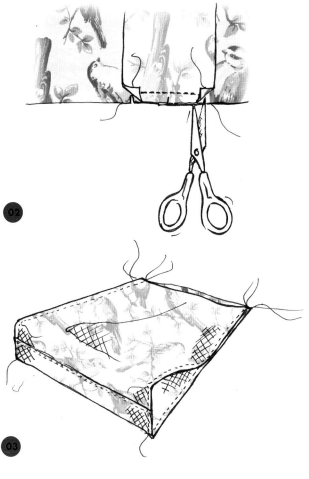

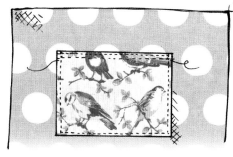

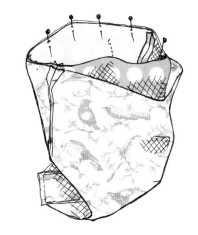

02 Lift up the unstitched corners and make two snips into the seam allowance of the bag panel, cutting to within $^1/_8$" [4 mm] of the seam line. This will enable the fabric to fit neatly around the corner.

Pin and baste the side edges of the bag panels to the edges of the side panel. Reinsert the needle at one end of the seam, work a couple of backstitches for security and machine stitch the seam from the base to the top edge.

03 Join the other side seam in the same way, then add the second side panel. Leave the bag wrong-side out.

SEW THE POCKET TO THE LINING

Press under a $^3/_8$" [1 cm] turning along the side and bottom edges of the pocket. Finish the top edge with a double $^3/_8$" [1 cm] turning, baste it down and secure the hem with two rows of machine stitching, $^1/_8$" [4 mm] and $^1/_4$" [6 mm] from the edge.

04 Position the pocket centrally on one of the lining-fabric bag panels, $2^1/_2$" [6 cm] down from the top edge. Pin and baste it in place, then machine stitch the side and bottom edges, $^1/_8$" [4 mm] from the fold. Reinforce each end of the seam with a few backstitches.

PREPARE THE LINING

With right sides together, baste and pin the bottom edges of the two lining-fabric bag panels together. Machine stitch, leaving an 8" [20 cm] opening in the center of the seam. Press the seam allowance open, including the unstitched part, then add the side panels as for the main bag. Press the seams open and turn right-side out.

JOIN THE LINING TO THE BAG

05 Place the lining inside the main bag, matching up the four seams. Pin the two together around the top edge, then baste and machine stitch, taking a $^3/_8$" [1 cm] seam allowance. Press the seam allowance so that it lies over the lining fabric—this will give a firm edge to the opening. (You may find it easier to baste this in place instead, as shown on page 97 of the Handbag.)

Pull the bag through the opening in the lining to turn the whole thing right-side out. Slip-stitch the opening by hand, then push the lining back inside the bag.

tip... YOU CAN EASILY SCALE THIS BAG DOWN BY REDUCING THE SIZE OF THE PATTERN PIECES. IF YOU PREFER A LESS BOXY LOOK, YOU DON'T HAVE TO TOPSTITCH THE SIDE SEAMS.

Adjust the seam line so that it lies on the inside, $^3/_8$" [1 cm] below the top edge. Baste all the way around the opening, $^1/_3$" [8 mm] from the top edge. Working from the inside of the bag, machine stitch "in the ditch"—a quilting term that means "along the seam line."

TOPSTITCH THE EDGES

06 Fold each side edge in turn so that the seam lies at the outside edge and baste through all the layers— the main bag, the lining, and the seam allowances. Topstitch each edge in turn, stitching from the opening downward to $^3/_8$" [1 cm] from the bottom corner.

ADD THE HANDLES

07 Make the two handles from the strips of fabric, following the instructions on page 21. Pin one to the front of the bag so that the outside edges lie $3^1/_4$" [8 cm] in from the corners and the short ends are 2" [5 cm] down from the top edge. Baste securely in place, then box stitch down with squares of reinforcing stitches (see page 21). Sew on the other handle in the same way.

HANDBAG

If you've never made your own handbag, this is the project that might just inspire you to get started! It's very quick to stitch, all the seams are straight and the compact size means that it doesn't take much fabric. I paired a vivid floral print with a plain lining, but you can mix and match prints to create your own individual look.

MATERIALS & EQUIPMENT

36" x 24" [90 x 60 cm] of a medium-weight floral cotton, for the main fabric
36" x 20" [90 x 50 cm] of a medium-weight plain cotton, for the lining
Matching sewing thread
Sewing box (see page 8)
Sewing machine

SIZE

10¼" x 10¼" x 5½" [25 x 25 x 14 cm], excluding handles

CUTTING OUT

FROM MAIN FABRIC

- Two 15¾" [40 cm] squares, for the front and back
- Two 20" x 4" [50 x 10 cm] handle strips

FROM LINING FABRIC

- Two 15¾" x 11¾" [40 x 30 cm] rectangles, for the front and back

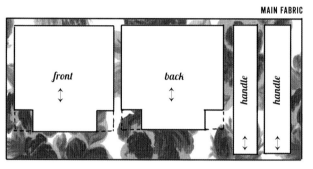

TO MAKE THE HANDBAG

SEW THE MAIN BAG PIECES TOGETHER

01 Cut out a 2¾" [7 cm] square from each bottom corner of each main-fabric square and each lining rectangle. With right sides together, pin the main front and back together along the side and bottom edges. Machine stitch these three seams, taking a ³⁄₈" [1 cm] seam allowance. Press the seams open.

Open out and refold the corners so that the side and bottom seams match up. Pin and machine stitch, taking a ³⁄₈" [1 cm] seam allowance. (You can find out more about T-junction seams on page 15.)

tip... DON'T WORRY ABOUT USING PALE COLORS, SIMPLY POP THE HANDBAG IN THE WASH, ON A COOL CYCLE. LAUNDERING WILL ALSO SOFTEN THE LOOK OF THE FABRIC AND ADD TO THE SLOUCHY, UNSTRUCTURED FEEL.

SEW THE LINING

02 Join the front and back in exactly the same way as the bag, but leave a 6" [15 cm] opening in the center of the bottom seam. Press the side seams open, and press back the seam allowances along both sides of the bottom edge, including the unstitched sections.

Finish off the corners with T-junction seams (see page 15) and turn the lining right-side out.

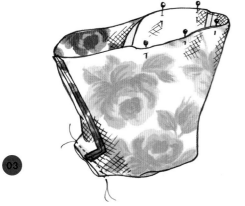

PUT IT ALL TOGETHER

03 Slip the lining inside the bag; the right sides should now be together. Match up the side seams and pin the two together all around the top opening. Machine stitch, taking a 3/8" [1 cm] seam allowance.

04 Baste the seam allowance down, so that it lies over the lining—you can do this by working with one hand through the opening, so that you don't catch any bag fabric with your needle. Turn the whole thing right-side out through the opening in the lining. Slip-stitch (see page 19) the folded edges of the seam allowance together to close the opening and push the lining inside the bag.

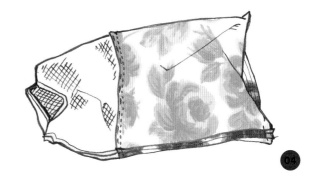

FINISH OFF THE TOP EDGE

05 Measure and baste down a 1³/₄" [4.5 cm] turning around the opening, using a tape measure or ruler to make sure that the depth is consistent. Machine stitch around the top edge of the lining, close to the basting stitches and ¹/₈" [4 mm] from the seam line. Press the top edge lightly for a crisp finish.

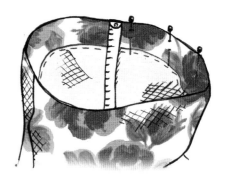

ADD THE HANDLES

06 Using the main-fabric handle strips, make the handles (see page 21). Pin them to the top edge, so that the outside edges lie 4" [10 cm] in from the corners and the short ends are lined up along the stitching line. Baste in place, then sew down securely with a box of reinforcing stitches (see page 21).

TAKE IT FURTHER

Change the look by using a pair of ready-made leather handles or two lengths of sturdy cotton tape instead of fabric strips.

Intermediate

CANVAS BAG

This practical bag is put together from cotton canvas, but it is made stylish with patterned handles. The same floral print fabric is used to add further touches of bright color to the pocket linings and the seam binding. The raw edges of the seams are finished with narrow strips of the floral fabric—a tailoring technique that has been borrowed to make the inside of the bag look as interesting as the outside.

CANVAS

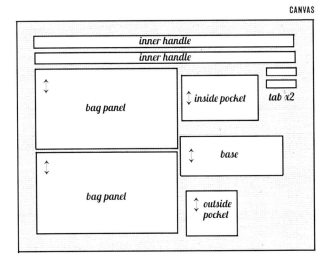

FLORAL PRINT FABRIC

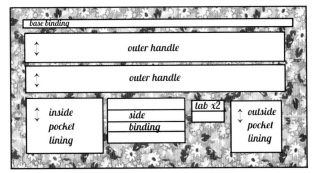

MATERIALS & EQUIPMENT

43" x 32" [110 x 80 cm] of unbleached canvas
43" x 20" [110 x 50 cm] of a floral cotton
Sewing thread to match canvas and floral print
One $^{1}/_{3}$" [8 mm] snap
Sewing box (see page 8)
Sewing machine
Size 16/100 (denim) machine needle

SIZE

Approximately 15$^{3}/_{4}$" x 6" x 11$^{3}/_{4}$" [40 x 15 x 30 cm]

CUTTING OUT

FROM CANVAS

- Two 22" x 11$^{3}/_{4}$" [55 x 30 cm] bag panels
- One 11$^{3}/_{4}$" x 8" [30 x 20 cm] inside pocket
- One 8" x 7$^{1}/_{4}$" [20 x 18 cm] outside pocket
- Two 39$^{1}/_{2}$" x 2" [100 x 5 cm] inner handle pieces
- One 15$^{3}/_{4}$" x 6" [40 x 15 cm] base
- Two 6" x 1$^{3}/_{8}$" [15 x 3.5 cm] tabs

FROM FLORAL FABRIC

- Four 11$^{3}/_{4}$" x 1$^{1}/_{4}$" [30 x 3 cm] side binding strips
- One 11$^{3}/_{4}$" x 8$^{3}/_{4}$" [30 x 22 cm] inside pocket lining
- One 8" [20 cm] square outside pocket lining
- One 41$^{1}/_{2}$" x 1$^{1}/_{2}$" [105 x 4 cm] base binding strip
- Two 6" x 1$^{3}/_{8}$" [15 x 3.5 cm] tabs
- Two 39$^{1}/_{2}$" x 5" [100 x 12 cm] outer handle pieces

FABRIC CHOICE

Unbleached canvas is a sturdy fabric that can be left unlined. It makes a good neutral background for the vintage mini print used on the handle here. A matching mini-print purse, adapting the pencil case pattern on page 128, would go with it very well.

Text inside diagram: inner handle (x2), bag panel (x2), inside pocket, tab x2, base, outside pocket, base binding, outer handle (x2), inside pocket lining, side binding, tab x2, outside pocket lining.

TAKE IT FURTHER

The two snap fastener tabs that are stitched to the side seams in the final step make this a versatile bag. When they are joined, the bag becomes a very different shape with a folded top—an idea that could be applied other tote bags.

TO MAKE THE CANVAS BAG

PREPARE THE BAG PANELS

Mark the handle positions on both canvas bag panels by drawing a vertical line 6" [15 cm] in from each side edge, using a fading fabric marker pen. Bind the side edges of the bag panels with the four floral side binding strips (see how to do this on page 17).

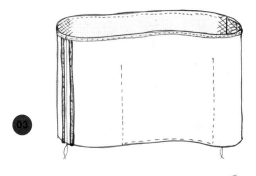

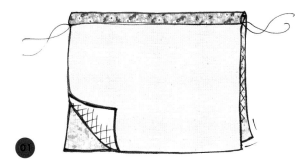

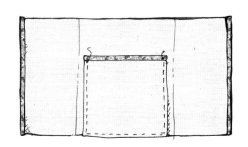

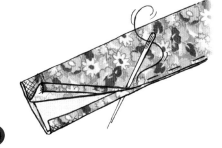

PREPARE THE POCKETS

The inside and outside pockets are both made in the same way. With right sides together, pin and baste the top edges of the lining and the pocket together. Machine stitch, taking a $^3/_8$" [1 cm] seam allowance.

01 Press the seam allowance to one side so that it lies over the lining, then turn the lining over to the back of the pocket: you'll now have a narrow floral band along the top edge of the front. Baste the side and bottom edges together, then press the top edge lightly.

02 Pin and baste the outside pocket centrally to the front of one bag panel, matching the lower edges.

JOIN THE BAG PANELS

Pin the two canvas bag panels together along the side edges, with right sides together. Machine stitch, taking a $^5/_8$" [1.5 cm] seam allowance, and press the seams open.

03 Press $^1/_4$" [6 mm] to the wrong side around the top edge and then press a second $^1/_2$" [12 mm] turning to make a double hem. Baste, then machine stitch close to the fold. Turn the bag right-side out.

MAKE THE HANDLES

04 Press under a $^3/_8$" [1 cm] turning along each long edge of an outer handle strip, then press it in half lengthwise. Tuck an inner handle under the bottom turning, then fold the outer handle over to cover the canvas. Baste together through all the layers. Machine stitch $^1/_8$" [4 mm] from each long edge, using thread to match the floral fabric.

Mark a point 15$^3/_4$" [40 cm] in from each end with a pin. Fold the handle in half, then pin and baste the long edges together between the pins. Machine stitch over the existing stitching line, reinforcing both ends of the seam for strength. Make the other handle in the same way.

SEW THE HANDLES TO THE BAG

Pin one of the handles to the bag front, with the center fold facing outward and the outside edges along the drawn-on lines. The inside edges will now cover the side edges of the pocket. Baste the handle securely in place.

05 Machine stitch the edges of the handle onto the bag and work an extra square of reinforcing stitches just below the top hem (see page 21). Join the other handle to the back of the bag in the same way.

ADD THE INSIDE POCKET

06 Turn the bag inside out. Press under a $^3/_8$" [1 cm] turning along the side edges of the inner pocket, then pin and baste it centrally to the back panel; the side edges will lie just beyond the handles. Machine stitch the side edges close to the folds, using thread to match the canvas.

JOIN ON THE BASE

Working on the wrong side, draw a $^3/_8$" [1 cm] seam allowance along each edge of the base with a fading fabric pen, then mark the center of the two short edges. With right sides together, pin these center points to the side seams of the bag. Pin the side edges of the base to the bag, leaving the seam allowance open at each corner.

07 Make two $^1/_4$" [6 mm] vertical snips into the seam allowance at each of these corner points, so that the seam allowance will open out around the corners. Pin the long edges of the base to the bag and baste securely in place. Machine stitch in place, taking a $^3/_8$" [1 cm] seam allowance. Bind the seam allowances with the base binding strip.

MAKE AND ADD THE TABS

Press under a $^3/_8$" [1 cm] turning at the short ends of the canvas tabs, then press under a $^3/_8$" [1 cm] turning along each long edge. Do the same with the floral fabric tab. With wrong sides together, pin and baste the two together, then machine stitch close to the edge of the floral fabric.

08 Fix the recessed part of the snap to the end of one tab, on the canvas side. Fix the other part to the floral side of the second tab. With the floral sides facing upward, sew one tab to the top of each side seam, just below the hem.

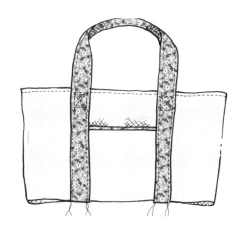

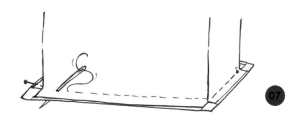

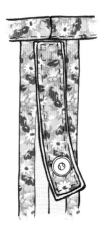

YOGA MAT BAG

This practical cylinder bag features a secure drawstring at the top edge and a carrying handle to sling over your shoulder, and introduces a useful technique—sewing a circle onto a cylinder with a curved seam. Once you have mastered this, you'll be able to make gathered bags in any shape and size (like the Backpack on page 142), or even a bolster or pillow.

MATERIALS & EQUIPMENT

TEMPLATE ON PAGE 155

32" x 28" [80 x 70 cm] of a medium-weight floral cotton, for the bag

32" x 27" [80 x 70 cm] of a lightweight plain cotton, for the lining

32" [80 cm] of sturdy cotton tape, 1^1/$_2$" [4 cm] wide

24" [60 cm] of cotton cord, ^{1}/$_4$" [6 mm] in diameter

Spring toggle fastening

Matching sewing thread

Small safety pin

Sewing box (see page 8)

Sewing machine

Size 16/100 (denim) machine needle

SIZE

The bag fits a standard mat that measures 24" x 15^3/$_4$" [60 x 40 cm] when it's rolled up tightly. If your mat is a different size, you will need to make the bag longer or wider and increase or reduce the size of the base.

CUTTING OUT

FROM FLORAL FABRIC

- One 20" x 25^1/$_2$" [50 x 65 cm] rectangle, for the main-bag piece
- One 20^1/$_2$" x 2^1/$_2$" [52 x 6 cm] gathering channel
- One 7" [17 cm] circle, for the base
- Four tabs (cut using template)

FROM LINING FABRIC

- One 20" x 25^1/$_2$" [50 x 65 cm] rectangle, for the main-bag piece
- One 7" [17 cm] circle, for the base
- One 2^1/$_4$" x 2^1/$_4$" [6 x 6 cm] reinforcing patch

FABRIC CHOICE

Yoga mats come in limited colors, so it's worth considering the color of yours before choosing your fabric. The long, thin shape of the bag is well-suited to large, bold prints.

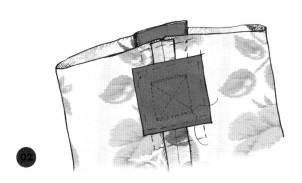

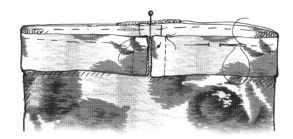

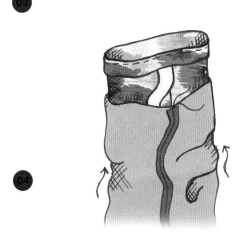

TAKE IT FURTHER

Instead of using a length of cotton tape, you can make a matching strap from a 31" x 4" [80 x 10 cm] strip of the bag fabric (see how to do this on page 21).

TO MAKE THE YOGA MAT BAG

PREPARE THE MAIN-BAG PIECE

Fold the floral main-bag piece in half widthwise, with the right sides together. Pin and baste the two side edges together to make a cylinder. Machine stitch, taking a $^3/_8$" [1 cm] seam allowance. Press the seam open and turn the cylinder right-side out.

01 Pin the ends of the cotton tape centrally across the top and bottom ends of the seam. Baste $3^5/_8$" [8 cm] of the tape to the bag at the top end. Turn the bag wrong-side out again. Draw a $1^3/_8$" [3 cm] square inside the small reinforcing patch and then draw two diagonal lines across the square from corner to corner. Lay the patch centrally across the seam, $1^1/_4$" [3 cm] down from the top edge, then baste it in place, stitching through the tape on the other side.

02 Using a sturdy denim needle so that you can sew easily through all the layers of fabric, machine stitch over the drawn lines. Turn the bag right-side out once again.

ADD THE GATHERING CHANNEL

Press under and stitch down a $^3/_4$" [2 cm] hem at each short end of the gathering channel, then press it in half lengthwise. Fold the strip in half the other way and mark the center point with a pin.

03 With right sides together, pin and baste the channel around the top end of the bag, lining up the raw edges and matching the center pin to the seam line at the back of the bag.

SEW IN THE LINING

Pin and baste the side edges of the lining main-bag piece together to make a cylinder, as you did for the floral bag. Machine stitch, taking a $^3/_8$" [1 cm] seam allowance, then press the seam open.

04 Slip the lining over the bag, so that the right side of the lining faces the right side of the bag, and match up the two seams at the top edge. Pin and baste all the layers together, then machine stitch around the opening, taking a $^3/_8$" [1 cm] seam allowance. Fold back the lining so that it is right-side out and push the main bag back through the opening: the gathering channel will now project above the top edge and the main bag will be inside the lining tube, wrong sides together. Press the top edge lightly. Baste the lining and bag together around the bottom edge.

ADD THE BASE
Pin the circle of lining fabric to the wrong side of the floral bag base and baste the two together around the outside edge. With right sides together, pin and baste the base to the bottom of the bag (see page 15).

05 With the cylinder uppermost, machine stitch twice around the outside edge for a strong seam, taking a $3/8$" [1 cm] seam allowance. Finish off the raw edges with a zigzag or overlocking stitch. (If you are a real perfectionist, you can cover them with bias binding instead.) Turn the bag right-side out for the last time.

THREAD THE DRAWSTRING
Fasten a small safety pin to one end of the cotton cord. Push the pin through the opening in the gathering channel, then ease it all the way around and back out again. Push down the button on the spring toggle and thread both ends through the central hole.

ADD THE FINISHING TOUCHES
06 Pin the tabs together in pairs, with the right sides together. Machine stitch $3/8$" [1 cm] from the side and bottom edges, leaving the top edge open. Trim the seam allowance to about $1/8$" [4 mm], turn both tabs right-side out, and ease out the corners. Tuck under a $3/8$" [1 cm] turning around the top edge and press lightly. Pop one tab over the end of each cord and sew the top edge securely in place by hand or by machine.

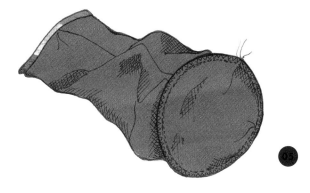

***tip*... IF THE ENDS OF YOUR CORD BECOME FRAYED, BIND EACH ONE TIGHTLY WITH ADHESIVE TAPE SO THEY WILL PASS EASILY THROUGH THE TOGGLE.**

GYM BAG

Lightweight and easy to fold away when empty, this unlined, zip-up bag is stylish, surprisingly roomy, and practical enough to carry all of your gym clothes.

MATERIALS & EQUIPMENT

43" x 34" [110 x 85 cm] of a medium-weight cotton print
2$\frac{1}{2}$ yards [213 cm] of sturdy striped cotton tape,
  1$\frac{1}{2}$" [4 cm] wide, for the handles
19$\frac{3}{4}$" [47 cm] zipper
Matching sewing thread
Sewing box (see page 8)
Sewing machine
16/100 (denim) machine needle

SIZE

19" x 9$\frac{1}{4}$" [48 x 23 cm] in diameter, excluding handles

CUTTING OUT

- One 19$\frac{3}{4}$" x 31$\frac{1}{2}$" [50 x 80 cm] rectangle, for the bag panel
- Two 2$\frac{1}{2}$" x 4" [6 x 10 cm] tabs
- Two 10" [25 cm] circles, for the round ends

FABRIC CHOICE

Adding the cheerful striped cotton tape gave this project added character, setting it apart from store-bought gym bags. Big bold vintage prints suit the shape of the bag. I picked out this fifties floral curtain print for its painterly look and was pleased to find a striped cotton tape for the handles that really highlights the bright red roses.

TO MAKE THE GYM BAG

PREPARE THE MATERIALS

Pin the two ends of the striped cotton tape together, making sure that the loop isn't twisted. Using a denim needle, machine stitch $\frac{3}{4}$" [2 cm] from the ends. Press the seam open. Finish the long top and bottom edges of the bag panel with a zigzag or overlocking stitch, then press under a $\frac{3}{8}$" [1 cm] turning along both these edges. Press and then unfold a 6" [15 cm] turning along each side edge: these creases mark the cotton tape positions. Insert two pins on each crease line, 3$\frac{1}{2}$" [9 cm] in from the top and bottom edges.

JOIN THE STRIPED TAPE TO THE BAG PANEL

Spread the bag panel out on a flat surface and place the striped tape loop lengthwise across it, with the seam line roughly at the left of center, facing downward. Starting at the seam line, position the inside edge of the striped tape along the crease and pin it down as far as the top left marker pin.

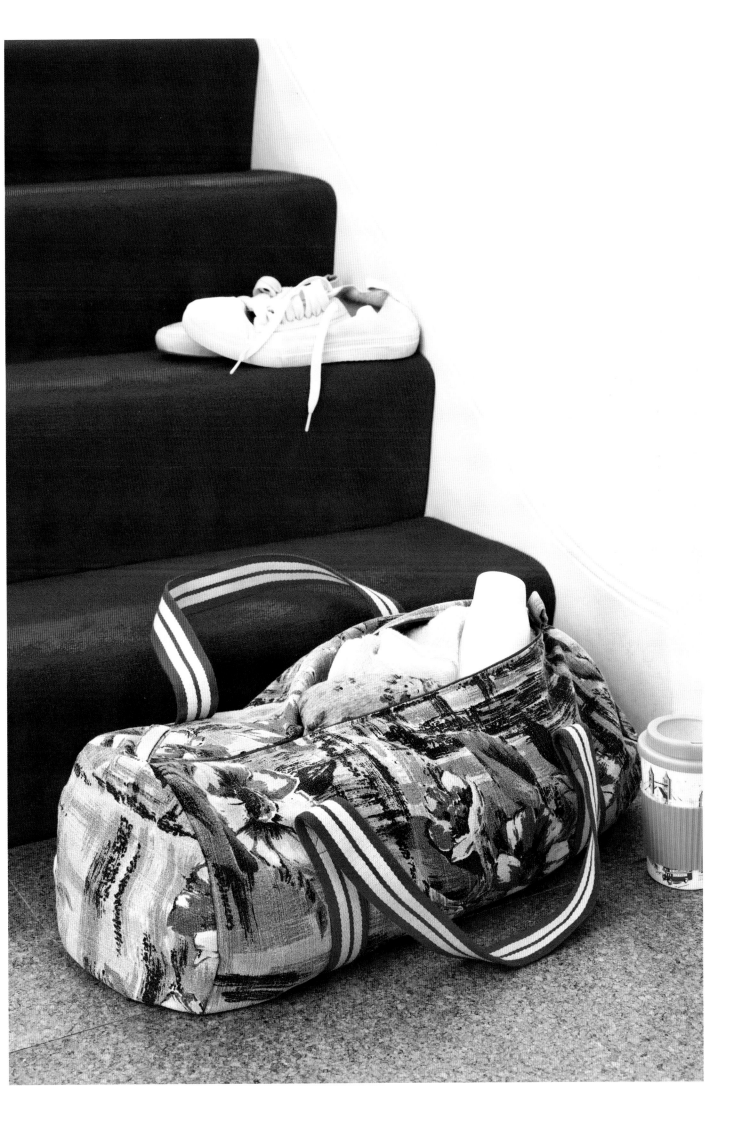

01 Measure 21³/₄" [55 cm] along the loop and insert a pin at this point to mark the length of the handle. Matching the pin with the top right marker pin, lay the inside edge of the tape along the right-hand crease and pin it as far as the bottom right marker pin. Pin the left part of the loop in the same way.

02 Baste the tape securely in place and stitch it along each edge with matching sewing thread. Sew a reinforcement square (see page 21) at the bottom of each handle to strengthen the handles.

ADD THE ZIPPER

Place the bag panel right-side down on your work surface. Center the zipper right-side down on the top edge of the bag panel, with the lower row of zipper teeth just beyond the fold. Partially close the zipper. Using a zipper foot, sew the zipper in place, ¹/₄" [6 mm] from the fold (see page 20). Sew the other side of the zipper tape to the bottom edge of the bag panel in the same way.

COMPLETE THE BAG

03 Fold the tabs in half lengthwise, with right sides together. Pin and machine stitch ³/₈" [1 cm] from the long edge. Turn right-side out, press, and fold in half widthwise. Baste one tab across each end of the zipper with the raw edges matching, using two big cross-stitches.

Sew the round ends to the bag panel (see page 15). Finish the seam allowances with zigzag or overlocking stitch, then turn the bag right-side out.

TAKE IT FURTHER

Altering the proportions of this zipped cylinder is very straightforward, which means the bag can be made up in almost any size. All you need is a calculator and some basic geometry. Decide on the diameter of the round ends (the height of the finished bag) and add on a ³/₄" [2 cm] seam allowance. Multiply this distance by 3.1 to find the circumference. Add a ³/₄" [2 cm] seam allowance to this figure and you have the length of the bag panel.

HOLDALL

This is one of those classic bags. It's just the right size and shape to be a baby's changing bag, picnic bag, or to hold all of your knitting and sewing projects. There are six roomy pleated pockets—three at the front, a taller one at each side and a wide back section. Making the bag is a good way to practice sewing seams, especially as there are no curves or sharp corners to deal with. Pin and baste each seam accurately and stitch slowly when you are working with more than two layers to keep the seam allowance even.

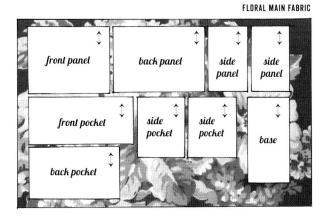

FLORAL MAIN FABRIC

LINING FABRIC

MATERIALS & EQUIPMENT

57" x 39" [145 x 100 cm] of a medium-weight floral cotton, for the main fabric

57" x 39" [145 x 100 cm] of a medium-weight plain cotton, for the lining

Matching sewing thread

49" [125 cm] of sturdy cotton tape, $1^1/2$" [4 cm] wide

Sewing box (see page 8)

Sewing machine

Size 16/100 (denim) machine needle

SIZE

15" x $11^3/4$" x 7" [40 x 30 x 20 cm]

CUTTING OUT

FROM FLORAL MAIN FABRIC

- Two $15^3/4$" x $12^3/4$" [40 x 32 cm] front and back panels
- Two $7^3/4$" x $12^3/4$" [20 x 32 cm] side panels
- One $20^1/2$" x $9^1/2$" [52 x 24 cm] front pocket
- One $17^1/4$" x $9^1/2$" [44 x 42 cm] back pocket
- Two $9^1/2$" x 11" [24 x 28 cm] side pockets
- One 8" x $16^1/4$" [20 x 40 cm] base

FROM PLAIN LINING FABRIC

- One $20^1/2$" x $9^1/4$" [50 x 23.5 cm] front pocket lining
- One 20" x $9^1/4$" [50 x 23.5 cm] back pocket lining
- Two $9^1/2$" x $10^3/4$" [24 x 27.5 cm] side pocket linings
- Two $22^3/4$" x $16^1/2$" [58 x 42 cm] panels, for front and back

FABRIC CHOICE

I chose thick cotton for the outside of the bag and the pockets and a plain canvas for the lining. This means that the sides of the bag are thick enough to stand up by themselves and the bag will hold its shape when full. Any similar-weight furnishing fabric would work here. To make it simpler, choose a dense pattern with an all-over print, so there is no need to match up the design on the panels and the pockets.

tip... YOU'LL BE SEWING THROUGH SEVERAL LAYERS OF THICK FABRIC, SO REMEMBER TO ATTACH A DENIM NEEDLE TO YOUR MACHINE BEFORE YOU START.

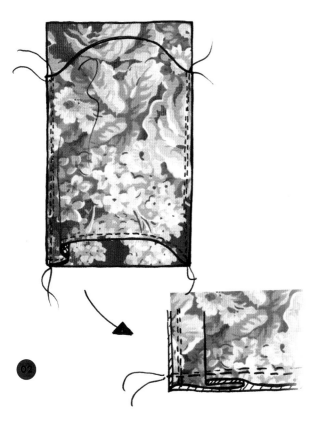

TO MAKE THE HOLDALL

LINE THE POCKETS

With the right side facing inward, pin and baste the top edge of a side pocket to a side pocket lining. Machine stitch, taking a $^3/_8$" [1 cm] seam allowance. Press the seam allowance so that it lies across the lining. Sewing from the right side and using thread to match the lining fabric, topstitch (see page 15) the lining $^1/_8$" [4 mm] from the seam.

01 Line up and pin together the bottom edges of the lining and main fabric, with the wrong sides together: there will now be a narrow margin of the main fabric along the top edge of the lining. Pin the sides together, then machine stitch all three pinned edges, taking a $^1/_8$" [4 mm] seam allowance.

Prepare the other side pocket and the larger front and back pockets in the same way. Press each one lightly.

PREPARE THE SIDE AND BACK PANELS

With the right sides facing upward, pin the left and right edges of one side pocket to the edges of one side panel. Machine stitch, sewing over the previous lines of stitching. The pocket is $1^1/_2$" [4 cm] wider than the panel and this extra fullness will be folded over to give it depth.

02 Make a $^3/_8$" [1 cm] pleat, $^3/_4$" [2 cm] in from the side edge at the bottom left corner, and baste it down. Do the same at the bottom right corner, then machine stitch across the bottom edge, once again stitching over the existing seam line.

Put together the other side panel and pocket, and the back panel and pocket in the same way.

PREPARE THE FRONT PANEL

The front pocket is pleated and stitched to make three separate divisions. Using tailor's chalk, draw a vertical line on the right side of the pocket, 7" [17 cm] in from each side edge: these will be the stitching lines. Lightly mark two lines on the right side of the bag front panel, 5$\frac{1}{4}$" [13.5 cm] in from each side edge.

03 Match the chalk lines on the pocket to the lines on the front panel. Pin and then baste the two together, close to the lines. Machine stitch along the chalk marks, reinforcing the top ends by stitching backward and forward three times for a distance of about $\frac{3}{4}$" [2 cm]. Pin, baste, and stitch the side edges together, taking a $\frac{1}{4}$" [6 mm] seam allowance.

04 Pleat and baste the bottom corners in the same way as for the other pockets, then make a $\frac{3}{8}$" [1 cm] pleat on each side of the two division lines. Secure the pleats by sewing all the way along the bottom edge, once again going over the existing stitching line.

SEW THE MAIN BAG TOGETHER

05 With the pockets facing inward, pin and baste the two side panels to the front panel. Machine stitch together from top to bottom, taking a $\frac{3}{8}$" [1 cm] seam allowance. Stop stitching $\frac{5}{8}$" [1.5 cm] before the end of the seam and reinforce both ends of the seam with a few backstitches. Add the back panel in the same way. Slide the bag over your ironing board and carefully press the seams open.

06 With right sides together, pin and baste the base to the bag. The unstitched seam allowance at the bottom corners will open out and lie flat against the base. With the bag uppermost, machine stitch all the way around the base, taking a $\frac{5}{8}$" [1.5 cm] seam allowance. Reinforce the corners with extra stitches. Clip a small triangle from each corner, cutting $\frac{3}{16}$" [5 mm] away from the stitching line.

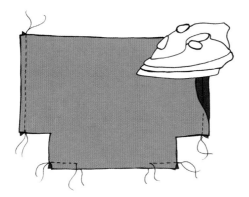

PREPARE THE BAG LINING

07 Cut a 3¹/₄" [8 cm] square from the two bottom corners of each bag lining. Pin the two pieces together along the side and bottom edges. Machine stitch the sides, taking a ³/₈" [1 cm] seam allowance, then sew a 1¹/₄" [3 cm] seam at each end of the bottom edge, reinforcing both ends with a few backstitches. Press the seams open, including the unstitched seam allowance on either side of the large center opening.

Now refold the corners so that the side and bottom seams are aligned, making a "T-junction" (see page 15). Pin and baste the two straight edges together and machine stitch, taking a ³/₈" [1 cm] seam allowance.

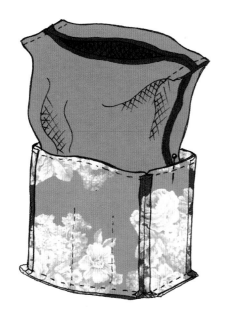

PUT IT ALL TOGETHER

08 Mark the center top edges of the sides of the main bag with pins. Matching these two pins to the side seams on the lining, and with the right sides facing inward, pin and baste the bag and lining together all the way around the top edge. Machine stitch, taking a ³/₈" [1 cm] seam allowance. Now turn the whole thing right-side out through the opening in the lining: you'll have to do a bit of wrestling to do this, but it will work!

Slip-stitch the folded edges together to close the opening and push the lining inside the bag. Lightly press the top edge.

ADD THE HANDLES

09 Cut the cotton tape in half and baste under a ³/₈" [1 cm] turning at each end of both pieces. Pin and baste the ends of the first piece to the front of the bag so that they overlap the top edge by 2¹/₂" [6 cm] and lie 2³/₄" [7 cm] in from the corners. Slowly and carefully sew the handle to the bag with two squares of reinforcing stitches (see page 21). Join the second handle to the back of the bag in the same way.

LUGGAGE TAG

We've all tried to find our bag in that great sea of suitcases. A bright fabric tag is a great way to identify your luggage. It's quick to make and, as long as you fold all the corners neatly and accurately, the finished look is surprisingly professional.

MATERIALS & EQUIPMENT

TEMPLATE ON PAGE 154

14" x 8" [35 x 20 cm] of a medium-weight cotton print

10" x 6" [25 x 15 cm] of medium-weight iron-on interfacing

Matching sewing thread

2$\frac{1}{2}$" x 4" [6 x 10 cm] piece of clear plastic

Metal eyelet, $\frac{5}{16}$" [8 mm] in diameter, and eyelet kit

10" [25 cm] of cord, $\frac{1}{8}$" [4 mm] in diameter

Double-sided tape

Sewing box (see page 8)

Sewing machine

Size 16/100 (denim) machine needle

SIZE

Approximately 5$\frac{3}{4}$" x 3" [14.5 x 7.5 cm]

CUTTING GUIDE

FROM INTERFACING (SEE PAGE 116)

- Two complete tag shapes
- One window-frame shape

FABRIC CHOICE

We used a mini floral print as it complements the large-scale flowers of the holdall, but the brighter the print, the better, to make your bag more distinctive.

TO MAKE THE LUGGAGE TAG

PREPARE THE INTERFACING

Trace the outer outline of the tag template on page 154 onto a sheet of paper and then cut it out. Using a sharp, soft pencil and the template, draw the shape twice onto the non-adhesive side of the interfacing. Now cut out the window-frame section of the template and use it to draw the window frame on the interfacing. Cut all three shapes from the interfacing.

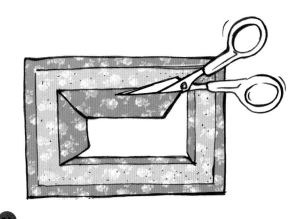

01

PREPARE THE WINDOW FRAME

01 Place the interfacing window-frame shape on the wrong side of your fabric, lining it up on the straight grain of the fabric. Press it in place, following the manufacturer's instructions, then cut out, leaving $^5/_{16}$" [7 mm] extra all around the outside edge. Snip into the center of the window, then cut diagonally up to each corner of the window. Trim the surplus fabric inside the window back to $^5/_{16}$" [7 mm].

02 Fold back and baste the seam allowance on the inside and outside of the window frame.

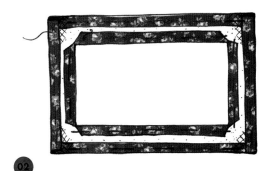

02

tip... THE CLEAR WINDOW AT THE FRONT OF THE TAG IS CUT FROM AN OLD DOCUMENT BINDER, BUT YOU CAN USE ANY SIMILAR CLEAR, FLEXIBLE PLASTIC.

03 Using a denim needle, machine topstitch $1/8$" [4 mm] from the inside and outside edges of the window frame. Using narrow strips of double-sided tape, attach the clear plastic to the wrong side.

ASSEMBLE THE TAG

04 Press the two interfacing tag shapes, adhesive side down, onto the back of the remaining fabric, leaving $3/8$" [1 cm] free around each one. Cut them out, leaving $5/16$" [7 mm] extra around each shape. Fold the seam allowance over to the interfacing side of the tags and baste it down.

05 Pin the two tag shapes wrong sides together, carefully matching up the corners. Now pin the window frame (right-side up) to the front and baste through all three layers, making sure that they don't shift. Topstitch slowly and carefully all the way around the outside edge of the tag, working a few backstitches at each corner of the window-frame to reinforce the join.

06 Attach a metal eyelet to the center top, $3/8$" [1 cm] in from the edge. Fold the cord in half and push the loop through the eyelet from front to back. Thread the ends through the loop and pull up tightly.

TAKE IT FURTHER

Writing a message on your luggage tag will turn it into a personal gift to tie onto a special parcel. You could reduce the template size and use a finer-weight fabric for a different look.

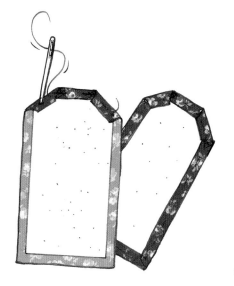

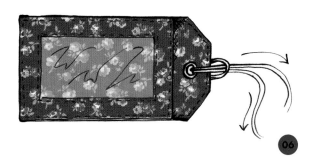

KIDS' STUFF

ENVELOPE PURSE

As you may have guessed, this sweet little bag is based on a simple folded envelope design. The outside and the lining are fused together with fusible adhesive web, which creates a firm, double-sided fabric that holds its shape well, and the edge is finished off with bias binding. You can make a very basic version of the purse as a starter project, but the scope for trims, buttons, and embellishments means that this is something you can really make your own.

MATERIALS & EQUIPMENT

TEMPLATE ON PAGE 158

10" x 10" [25 x 25 cm] piece of a lightweight floral cotton, for the main fabric

10" x 10" [25 x 25 cm] piece of a lightweight floral cotton, for the lining

10" x 10" [25 x 25 cm] piece of fusible adhesive web

1¼ yards [1 m] of bias binding, ½" [12 mm] wide

Sewing thread to match the binding and fabric

1¼ yards [1 m] of ribbon, ½" [12 mm] wide

One small button

Six-strand embroidery floss to match the fabric

Sewing box (see page 8)

Sewing machine

SIZE

Approximately 6" x 4½" [15 x 11 cm]

FABRIC CHOICE
Any of my bright floral prints would work well here, especially if you add a lining in a small-scale polka dot.

TO MAKE THE PURSE

PREPARE THE FABRIC
Following the manufacturer's instructions, press the adhesive side of the fusible adhesive web onto the wrong side of the main fabric. Peel off the backing paper. Place the fabric web side up on your ironing board, then lay the lining square wrong-side down on top. Match up the corners and press with a hot iron to fuse the two together.

CUT OUT THE ENVELOPE SHAPE
01 Trace the purse template on page 158 onto a large sheet of paper and cut it out. Pin it to the double layer of fabric (it doesn't matter which side) and draw around the edge with a fading fabric marker pen. Remove the template, then carefully cut around the outline.

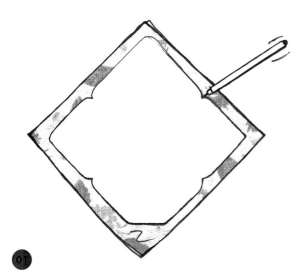

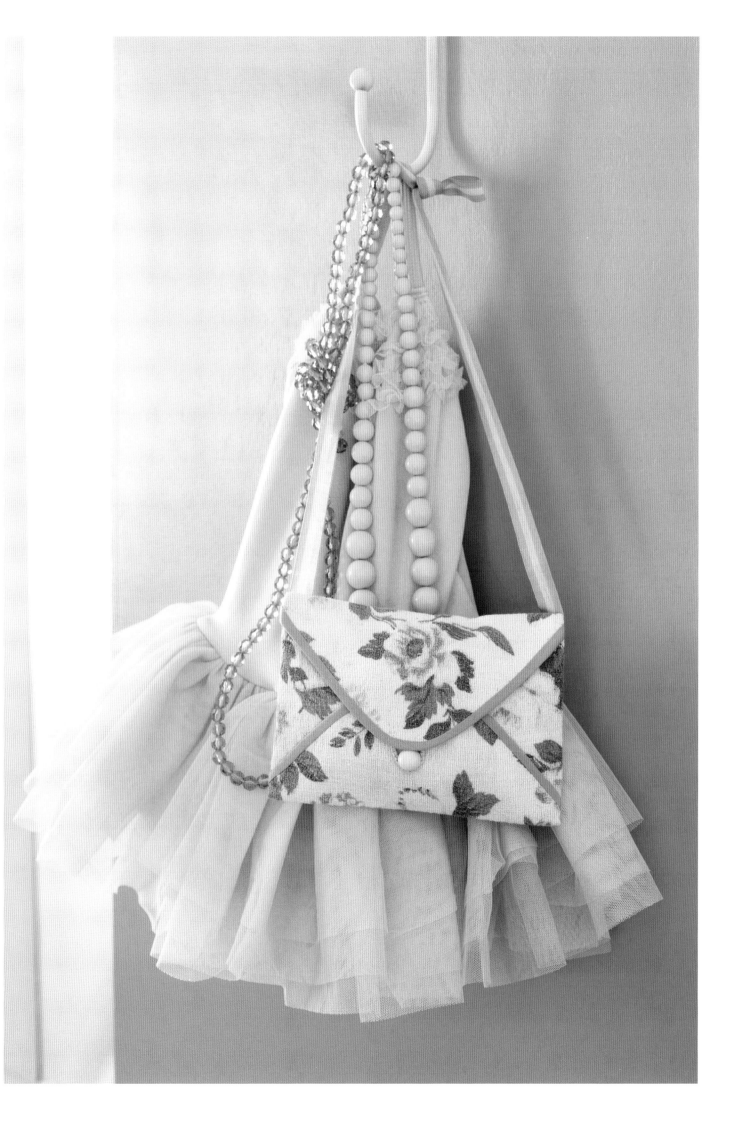

tip... MATCH YOUR BIAS BINDING AND RIBBON STRAP TO THE PREDOMINANT COLOR IN YOUR MAIN FABRIC FOR A COORDINATED LOOK OR PICK AN UNEXPECTED CONTRASTING SHADE.

BIND THE EDGE

02 Turn back the outside fold of the bias binding. Starting at the point marked A on the template, and with the main fabric facing upward, baste the raw edge of the binding around the edge of the envelope, stitching just inside the fold line (see page 17). You don't have to neaten the join, as it will be hidden when the envelope is sewn together. Ease the binding around the first curve.

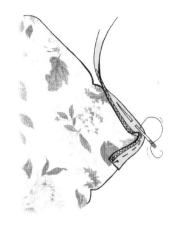

03 At the inside corners, make and baste a small pleat in the binding. Continue basting until you are back at A, and trim off the remainder of the binding. Machine stitch the binding to the fabric along the crease line. Turn the folded edge over to the back and slip-stitch it down.

SEW THE ENVELOPE TOGETHER

04 With the lining side facing upward, press the side edges in along the fold lines marked on the template. Press in the top and bottom edges, again following the marked lines.

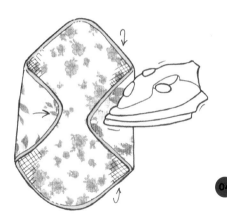

05 Pin the edges of the bottom flap to the side flaps. Using thread to match the fabric, work a line of small running stitches close to the inside edge of the binding, where the side and bottom flaps overlap, taking care not to stitch through to the back of the purse. Work a few extra stitches at the inside edge to reinforce the join.

ADD THE FINISHING TOUCHES

Press under a $1/4$" [6 mm] turning at each end of the ribbon, then hand stitch it securely to the back of the finished purse at the top corners.

Make a buttonhole loop at the point of the top flap, using three strands of embroidery floss (see page 20). Sew the button to the bottom flap so that it lies directly under the loop when the bag is closed.

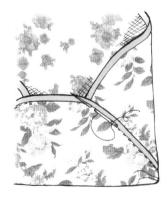

TAKE IT FURTHER

Maintain your green credentials by making a fabric envelope as a container for a hand-made birthday card or tiny present. Increase the size of the template for a larger version.

BOOK COVER

There's something rather special about a fabric-covered book, whether it's a journal, a reference book, or an old hardback edition of a favorite novel. For this project we chose a large-format diary covered in my London print, but the same method can be used to make a slip cover of any size, and is a good project to use up odd lengths of fabric. An individually selected book and cover also makes a thoughtful present.

MATERIALS & EQUIPMENT

A lightweight or medium-weight cotton print
Narrow ribbon, 6" [15 cm] longer than the height of the book
Matching sewing thread
Adhesive tape
Sewing box (see page 8)
Sewing machine

CUTTING OUT

- One pocket piece, width of book x height of book
- One cover panel, 5 x width of book x height of book + 2¹⁄₂" [6 cm]

TO MAKE THE BOOK COVER

SEW ON THE POCKET

01 Finish the right-hand edges of the cover panel and pocket piece with a ³⁄₈" [1 cm] single hem. Place the pocket right-side up on your work surface and lay the cover on top, so that the hem lies ³⁄₄" [2 cm] in from the pocket hem. Pin and baste the two together along the top and bottom edges.

CHECK THE FIT

02 Wrap the cover around the book, with the right side facing outward. Position the pocket edge ³⁄₄" [2 cm] in from the spine edge of the inside front cover and fold back the right-hand edge so that it lies ³⁄₈" [1 cm] from the spine edge of the inside back cover. Cut along this fold line and finish with a ³⁄₈" [1 cm] single hem.

tip... GIVE A HARDBACK BOOK A PADDED LOOK BY GLUING A RECTANGLE OF QUILT BATTING OVER THE COVERS AND THE SPINE BEFORE YOU MEASURE THE COVER.

tip... YOU CAN ALSO ADD A TITLE TO YOUR BOOK BY STITCHING A FELT OR FABRIC LABEL HOLDER TO THE FRONT COVER, JUST LIKE THE ONES ON OUR STORAGE CONTAINERS (PAGE 48).

SEW THE COVER TOGETHER

03 With the wrong side facing outward, wrap the cover around the book again, so that the side edges are ³/₄" [1 cm] in from the spine edge of the front and back covers. Baste the raw edges together along the top and bottom of both covers, close to the cover.

SEAM THE EDGES

04 Machine stitch all the way along the top and bottom edges, just outside the basting. Clip the corners to within ¹/₈" [4 mm] of the stitching and turn the cover right-side out. Ease out the corners and press lightly, pressing the seam allowances along the spine section to the wrong side.

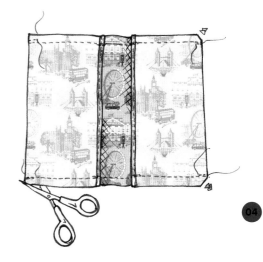

ADD THE BOOKMARK

05 Tape the ribbon to the center top of the book spine, on the outside of the book.

PUT ON THE FABRIC COVER

Fold the front and back covers of the book back as far as they will go and slide them into the fabric cover.

MAKE IT SIMPLER

If you're making a fabric cover for a novel, you won't need the pocket in the front flap, so just omit this step.

PENCIL CASE

A pencil case may be an everyday item, but it doesn't have to be ordinary, especially when it's made from a bright, illustrative print, which will appeal to children. You don't need a lot of fabric, so this is a quick make that you could put together in an afternoon from remnants or scraps from other projects.

MATERIALS & EQUIPMENT

24" x 8" [60 x 20 cm] of a medium-weight cotton print, for the main fabric
24" x 8" [60 x 20 cm] of a lightweight polka dot cotton, for the lining
10" [25 cm] zipper
Sewing thread to match both fabrics
11 1/2" [30 cm] of narrow cord
Three beads with large holes
Sewing box (see page 8)
Sewing machine

SIZE

10" x 6" [25 x 15 cm]

CUTTING OUT

Line up the two panels when you are cutting out the main fabric to match the repeat if necessary.

FROM MAIN FABRIC
- Two 10 3/4" x 6" [27 x 15 cm] panels

FROM LINING FABRIC
- Two 10 3/4" x 6" [27 x 15 cm] panels

FABRIC CHOICE

I used my Train print for the outside, but any medium-weight fabric would work well. You'll need a finer fabric for the lining, like my lightweight Mini Dot. Customize the zipper pull with any odds and ends you have at hand. Beads were used on the tassel shown here, but braided fabric, ribbon, or mini pompoms would also look fun.

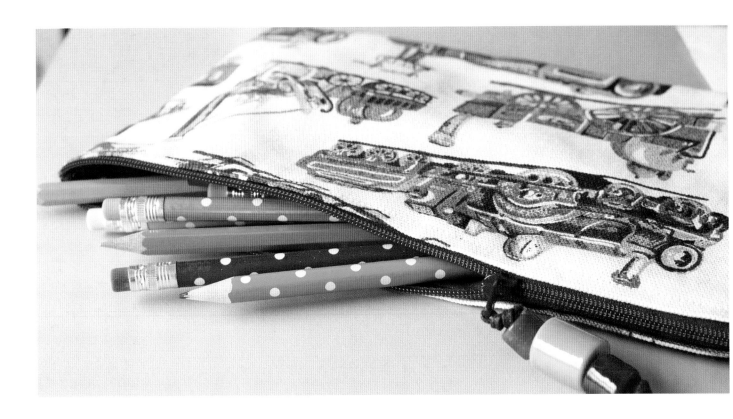

tip... YOU CAN GIVE YOUR PENCIL CASE MORE BODY, AND PAD IT OUT A BIT, BY SLIPPING A RECTANGLE OF QUILTER'S BATTING IN BETWEEN THE MAIN FABRIC AND THE LINING.

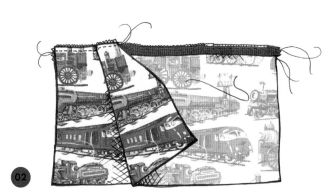

TO MAKE THE PENCIL CASE

SEW ON THE ZIPPER

Press 3/8" [1 cm] to the wrong side along the top edge of each main-fabric panel.

01 With the right side facing upward, pin the top edge of one panel centrally along the lower half of the zipper, so that the teeth just peep out above the fold. Baste the panel securely to the zipper tape. Using a zipper foot, machine stitch the zipper in place, stitching 1/4" [6 mm] from the fold. Sew the other main-fabric panel to the top half of the zipper in the same way. (You can find out more about sewing zippers on page 20.)

SEW THE PANELS TOGETHER

02 Open up the zipper and fold the two panels so that the right sides are facing inward and the corners are matched up. Pin and baste the side and bottom edges together, then machine stitch, taking a 3/8" [1 cm] seam allowance.

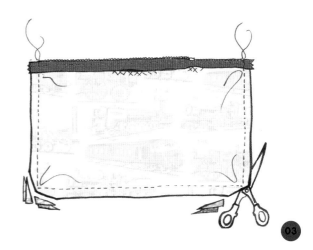

03 Reduce the bulk at the bottom corners by trimming a triangular sliver from each side. Press the seam allowances inward, then turn right-side out. Open the zipper fully.

ADD THE LINING

04 With right sides together, pin and baste the two lining panels together, then machine stitch, taking a $^3/_8$" [1 cm] seam allowance and leaving the top edge open. Trim the top and bottom corners as for the main panels. Press under $^3/_8$" [1 cm] along the top edges, then press the side and bottom seam allowances inward.

05 With wrong sides together, slip the lining inside the pencil case, matching up the seam lines. Push the bottom corners right down inside. Pin and baste the folded edge of the lining to the zipper tapes, so that it lies just above the stitching lines. Slip-stitch in place, using thread to match the lining. Sew as far into the ends as you can. If you're a real perfectionist, turn the case inside out to secure the inside corners.

KNOT THE TASSEL

06 Pass one end of the cord through the zipper pull and tie the ends together knot close to the pull. Thread on the beads. Keep them in place with another knot and trim the ends of the cord to $^3/_8$" [1 cm].

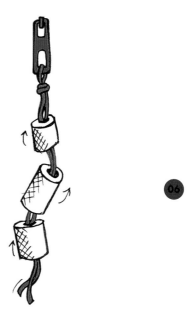

TAKE IT FURTHER

This design works for all manner of purses, meaning you can adapt this project to fit whatever you want. A long, thin bag—about 12" x 4" [30 x 10 cm]—would make a good knitting-needle holder, while a smaller 6" x 4" [15 x 10 cm] rectangle is the right shape for make-up essentials.

LUNCH BAG

There's lots of room inside this roll-top bag for a healthy packed lunch, so it's a good alternative to an ordinary plastic box. It's made from oilcloth fabric, and the rigidity of the vinyl coating gives it a strong, structured shape. It also means that you'll have to take a little extra care when sewing with this distinctive fabric—the hints below should help you achieve a professional finish.

MATERIALS & EQUIPMENT

32" x 16" [80 x 40 cm] of an oilcloth fabric, with a
   non-directional pattern
32" x 16" [80 x 40 cm] of a lightweight waterproof
   fabric (such as, woven shower curtain fabric)
2" [5 cm] of hook-and-loop tape, 1" [2.5 cm] wide,
   for the fastener
6" [15 cm] of sturdy cotton tape, 1" [2.5 cm] wide,
   for the strap
Matching sewing thread
Double-sided tape
Scallop-edged scissors or pinking shears
Masking tape
Sewing box (see page 8)
Sewing machine
Size 16/100 (denim) machine needle
Specialty machine foot (optional—see below)

SIZE

Approximately 8³/₄" x 4" x 12¹/₂" [22 x 10 x 32 cm]

CUTTING OUT

FROM OILCLOTH

- One 29¹/₂" x 10" [75 x 25 cm] main panel
- Two 5" x 11³/₄" [12 x 30 cm] side panels

FROM LINING FABRIC

- One 28³/₄" x 9" [73 x 23 cm] main panel
- Two 4" x 11¹/₂" [10 x 29 cm] side panels

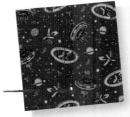

FABRIC CHOICE

While oilcloth is super practical, it is not armor-plated. Wipe it off but don't wash it, and be careful with spillages, as certain foods, such as vinegar, can eat into the print.

WORKING WITH OILCLOTH

There's no problem when you're stitching oilcloth from the wrong side, but the presser foot can't slide smoothly over the surface when the fabric is right-side up (when you are topstitching, for example). Unless you have a specialty roller foot, you will need to cover the smooth sole of your standard foot with a temporary layer of masking tape.

You should also use narrow lengths of masking tape to hold two pieces of oilcloth together instead of pins, which will pierce holes in the smooth surface. Use a polycotton thread and a size 16/100 (denim) needle for a strong seam. If your fabric has been left folded, you can get rid of the creases by leaving it in a warm place for a while; please don't be tempted to iron it to save time!

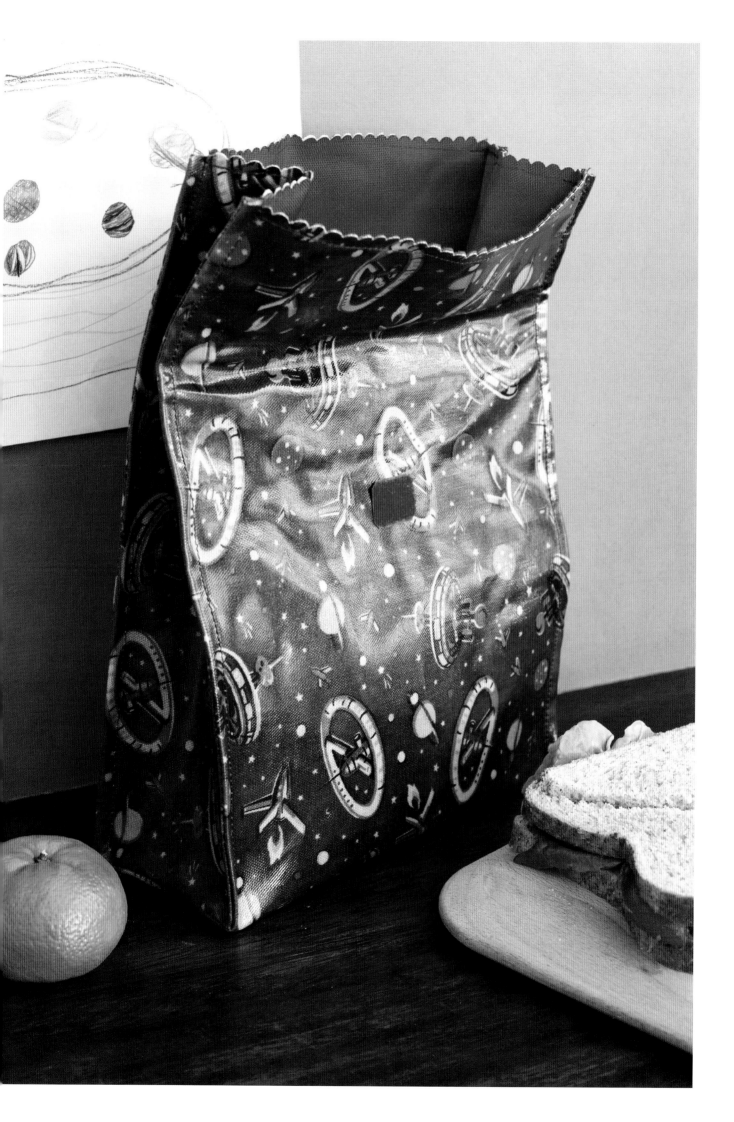

TO MAKE THE LUNCH BAG

JOIN ON THE FASTENER AND STRAP

01 Separate the two parts of the hook-and-loop fastener tape. Using double-sided tape, attach the looped part centrally to the right side of the oilcloth main panel, 8" [20 cm] in from one short edge, then machine stitch in place. Fold under and stitch down a 1/4" [6 mm] turning at each end of the cotton tape. Attach the hooked part of the hook-and-loop tape over one end with double-sided tape, so that it lies across the folded edge. Machine stitch, close to the edge of the hook-and-loop tape. Tape the other end of the cotton tape centrally to the oilcloth main panel, 6" [15 cm] in from the second short edge, with the hook-and-loop tape facing inward. Sew it down with a square of reinforcing stitches (see page 21).

MARK THE STITCHING LINES

With the right side facing inward, fold the main panel in half widthwise and mark the center point of each long edge on the wrong side of the oilcloth, using a pencil. Again drawing on the wrong side of the oilcloth, mark a 1/4" [6 mm] seam allowance along one short edge and both long edges of the side panels. Mark the center point on each short edge.

01

SEW THE BAG TOGETHER

With right sides together, match the center points of a side panel and the main panel. Tape the two together, 3/8" [1 cm] from the edge, then machine stitch along the pencil line at the bottom of the side panel, leaving the seam allowance unstitched at each end. Reinforce both ends of the seam with a few backstitches.

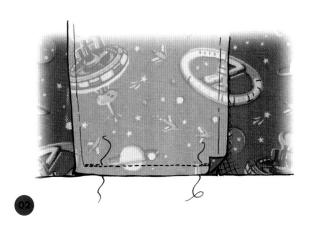

02

02 Lift up the bottom corners of the side panel and make a 3/16" [5 mm] snip into the seam allowance of the main panel, directly below each end of the seam.

tip... THE WRONG SIDE OF THE OILCLOTH CAN BE MARKED WITH A SHARP PENCIL, SO IT'S EASY TO DRAW YOUR SHAPES DIRECTLY ONTO THE FABRIC. USE AN OILCLOTH WITH A NON-DIRECTIONAL PATTERN: THE BACK AND FRONT ARE CUT IN ONE PIECE AND YOU DON'T WANT THE DESIGN TO BE UPSIDE DOWN!

03 Fold the bottom left-hand edge of the main panel upward at a right angle, so that it lies along the left-hand edge of the side panel. Stick them together with a few narrow strips of tape.

04 With the side panel uppermost, reinsert the machine needle at one end of the seam and stitch along the marked seam allowance to the top edge, again reinforcing both ends of the seam with backstitches. Join the main panel to the right-hand side panel edges in the same way, then add the second side panel.

Turn the finished bag right-side out and ease out the seams, using a pencil or knitting needle to square off the corners.

TOPSTITCH THE SEAMS

05 Pinch together the sides of each side seam, then topstitch down each seam in turn, stitching $1/3$" [8 mm] from the seam. Start from the top and sew downward, ending the seam about $3/8$" [1 cm] from the bottom corner. Work a few backstitches to secure, then trim the thread.

PUT IT ALL TOGETHER

Sew the lining pieces together in the same way, taking a $1/4$" [6 mm] seam allowance, but don't turn it right-side out or topstitch the sides. Finger press the seams open by flattening out the seam allowance between your fingers and thumbs—using an iron might melt the fabric!

06 Slip the lining inside the bag, pushing it right down inside. Tape the two layers together at intervals around the opening, but don't worry if they don't line up precisely. Machine stitch around the top of the main bag, $5/8$" [1.5 cm] down from the top edge, then trim the edge with pinking or scallop shears.

TAKE IT FURTHER

Omit the lining, finish the top edge with a double hem, and add two 12" [30 cm] handles to make this into an adorable tote bag.

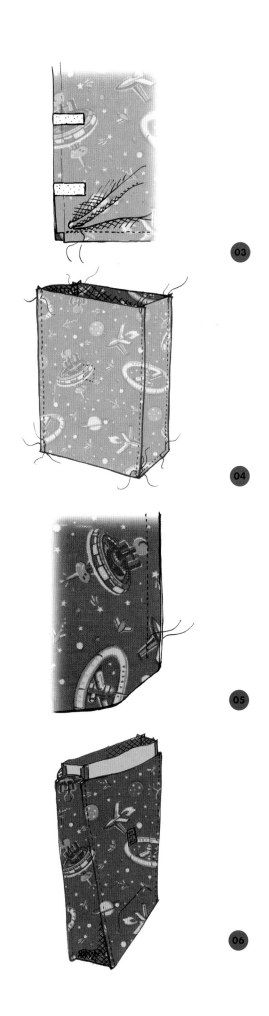

03

04

05

06

CROCODILE TOY

This graphic crocodile print seemed to be waiting to be made into a toy crocodile, but a textured plain green fabric, such as velours or corduroy, would be a fine alternative. Rickrack, which is ordinarily used as a pretty trimming, is perfect for his ridged back and ferocious teeth. Take care not to overstuff the body, as you want that squeezable, bean bag feel.

MATERIALS & EQUIPMENT

TEMPLATES ON PAGES 158 TO 159

22" x 14" [55 x 35 cm] of a medium-weight cotton print, for the main fabric

12" [30 cm] of green rickrack, $5/8$" [15 mm] wide

18" [25 cm] of white rickrack, $1/2$" [12 mm] wide

Scraps of white, green, and black felt

Matching sewing threads

$10^1/2$ ounces [300 g] of plastic toy filling beads (not suitable for children)

Small amount of safety-standard polyester toy filling

Sewing box (see page 8)

Sewing machine

SIZE

Approximately 10" x $5^1/2$" [25 x 14 cm]

CUTTING OUT

FROM MAIN FABRIC

- Two bodies, one reversed
- Transfer all of the markings onto the right-facing piece, and the eye and mouth positions to the other.

FROM FELT

- Two white eyes
- Two green eyelids
- Two black pupils

Warning!

SAFETY FIRST. Adorable as he may be, this toy isn't really suitable for babies or toddlers under 36 months. If you are going to give him to an older child, fill him with safety-standard polyester filling, embroider the eye in satin stitch and ensure that the rickrack and seams are sewn very securely.

TO MAKE THE TOY

ADD THE RICKRACK

01 Place the right-facing crocodile front on your work surface, with the right side of the fabric facing upward. Lay the green rickrack along his back between points A and B. Pin and baste it down so that the top edge lies along the edge of the fabric. Fold the raw ends upward so that they extend past the edge of the fabric.

02 Turn under $1/4$" [6 mm] at one end at one end of the white rickrack. With the folded end at C, baste it along the mouth, curving it to fit the line between C and D. Trim the end at D, in line with the raw edge. Sew both wavy edges down securely by hand, using white thread. Do the same on the other body piece.

03 The claws are made from short lengths of gathered white rickrack. Cut two pieces, each five "waves" long. Turn under and stitch down the last wave at each end. Pleating it so that the curves all point inward, baste the rickrack to each foot between points E and F on one body piece.

JOIN THE FRONT AND BACK

04 With right sides together, pin the two pieces together, carefully matching the feet, tail, and head. Baste, then machine stitch from point G all the way around the legs, tail, and head to point H, taking a 1/4" [6 mm] seam allowance and leaving the underbelly open. Press back the seam allowance along both sides of the opening. Trim the rest of the seam allowance back to 1/8" [4 mm] and clip into the curves (see page 15). Turn right-side out. Use a knitting needle or a blunt pencil to ease out the tail and toes.

STUFF THE TOY

05 Fill the body with the plastic beads, feeding them through the opening in the underbelly a teaspoonful at a time. Shake the beads down, then slip-stitch the opening securely to close it.

ADD THE EYES

06 Work a line of small running stitches around the outside edge of one white eye. Pull up the thread to gather the felt into a ball. Stuff firmly with toy filling, then fasten securely. Sew the back of the eye to one of the marked circles. Sew on the pupil and the hooded eyelid with matching thread, then stitch securely around the outside edge so that the eye sinks slightly into the head. Repeat on the other side.

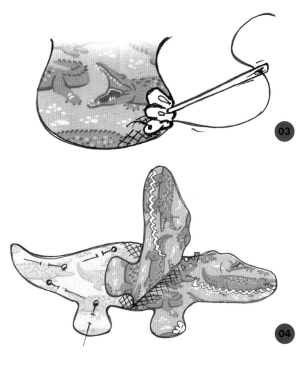

Easy

SPORT BAG

This simple and practical bag is perfect for holding your child's sports stuff. I chose our Dinosaur print here, but you could opt for a themed print, such as a vintage football or ballet scene, to match the contents. Only the most basic sewing skills are needed and all the seams are straight, so this is a good learning project for a beginner.

MATERIALS & EQUIPMENT

32" x 20" [80 x 50 cm] of a lightweight or medium-weight cotton print

Matching sewing thread

10" [25 cm] of cotton tape, $^1/_2$" [12 mm] wide

4 yards [3.5 m] of cord, $^1/_4$" [6 mm] in diameter

Large safety pin

Sewing box (see page 8)

Sewing machine

SIZE

$13^3/_4$" x $15^3/_4$" [35 x 40 cm]

CUTTING OUT

- Two $14^1/_2$" x $17^3/_4$" [37 x 45 cm] bag panels
- Two 2" x $1^1/_2$" [5 x 4 cm] tabs

TO MAKE THE SPORT BAG

ADD THE SIDE LOOPS

Turn under, press, and machine stitch a $^3/_8$" [1 cm] single hem along the top edge of each bag panel, then repeat along the side edges and the bottom edge.

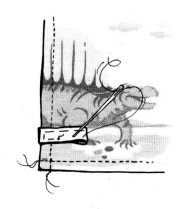

01 Place one bag panel right-side up on your work surface. Cut the woven tape in half, and fold one length to make a loop. Baste it to the left edge, $^3/_4$" [2 cm] up from the bottom corner, aligning the raw edges with the raw edge of the bag panel. Add the other tape to the bottom right corner in the same way.

SEW THE BAG PANELS TOGETHER

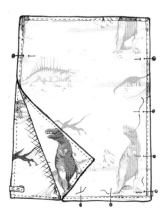

02 Place the second bag panel on top of the first, with right sides together, making sure that the pattern is the right way up. Measure 4" [10 cm] down from each top corner and mark these points with a pin. Pin and baste the panels together. Machine stitch around the sides and base, taking a $^3/_8$" [1 cm] seam allowance and leaving the side edges unstitched above the marker pins. Work two rows of extra stitches over the ends of the tapes to reinforce the loops.

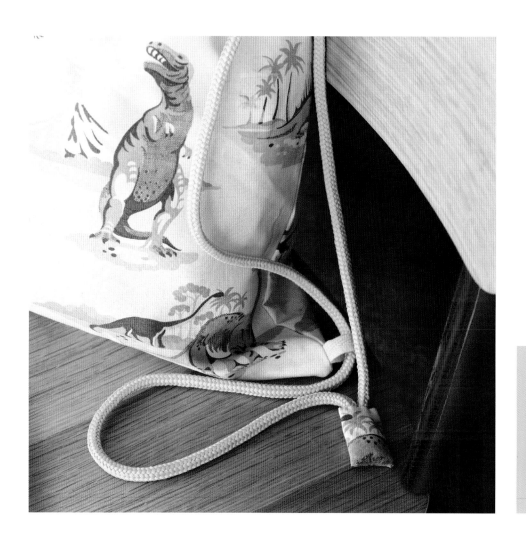

MAKE IT SIMPLER

Turn this project into a simple drawstring bag by reducing the length of the cords and omitting the loops at the bottom corners.

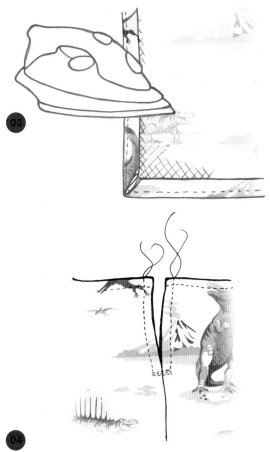

03 Cut away a small triangle from each bottom corner, snipping to within $1/8$" [4 mm] of the stitching line. Press the side and bottom seam allowances (including the unstitched seam allowances at the top edges) inward, over the bag panels. Turn the bag right-side out and press lightly.

PREPARE THE CORD CHANNEL

04 Baste down the unstitched seam allowance, then machine stitch, sewing $1/4$" [6 mm] from the folded edges and stitching three times across the seam line for extra strength.

05 Turn under and press a 2¹/₂" [6 cm] turning along each top edge. This creates the narrow channel for the cords. Pin and baste the turnings to the bag, then stitch them both down just inside the folded hemmed edges.

THREAD THE CORDS

06 Cut the cord in half and fasten a safety pin to the end of one length. Push it through the left side opening, feed it all the way around both channels, then back out of the opening. Slip one end through the left side loop. Thread the other cord through the right opening and the right side loop.

ADD THE TABS

07 Turn under and press a ¹/₄" [6 mm] turning along the top edge of each tab. Fold them in half widthwise, with right sides together, then baste and stitch the side and bottom edges, taking a ¹/₄" [6 mm] seam allowance. Clip a tiny triangle from each bottom corner and turn right-side out.

Trim the ends of the left-hand cord if they have become frayed and sew them securely together by hand. Slide one of the tabs over the joined ends and stitch the top edge to the cords. Do the same on the other cord.

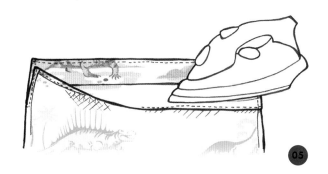

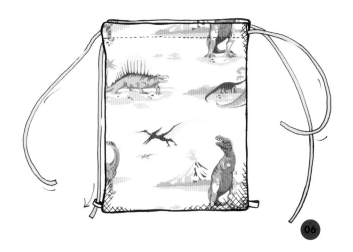

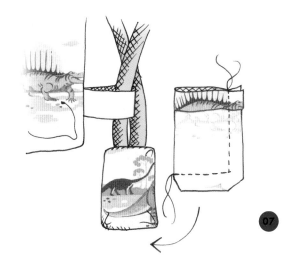

TAKE IT FURTHER

It's very easy to enlarge the rectangular panels for a laundry bag, or to make them smaller for a shoe bag. If you alter the proportions, you'll need to change the length of the cord. Whatever the size, you'll need a length that equals 4 x the top edge + 4 x the side edge + 4" [10 cm].

tip... YOU CAN GIVE THE TABS A PADDED LOOK BY WRAPPING THE ENDS OF THE CORD WITH TOY FILLING OR A SMALL RECTANGLE OF QUILT BATTING, BEFORE YOU SLIP ON THE COVERS.

FLORAL BACKPACK

There is always a healthy competition at school over having the coolest backpack. While the time and skill involved in stitching this project make it a true labor of love, the result is worth it: nobody will have the same design! Mix and match floral fabrics with polka dots, or use a combination of print and plain to give the bag a modern look.

MATERIALS & EQUIPMENT

TEMPLATE ON PAGE 154–155

Medium-weight fabric in three floral designs:
- 30" x 12" [75 x 30 cm] of floral cotton fabric 1
- 10" x 10" [25 x 25 cm] of floral cotton fabric 2
- 10" x 10" [25 x 25 cm] of floral cotton fabric 3

Medium-weight fabric in two polka dot designs:
- 42" x 28" [102 x 70 cm] of a pink polka dot cotton
- 10" x 10" [25 x 25 cm] of a red polka dot cotton

20" x 12" [50 x 30 cm] of polyester batting

Magnetic bag fastener, $5/8$" [15 mm] in diameter

Two buckles, with 1" [2.5 cm] wide openings

28" [70 cm] of sturdy cotton tape, 1" [2.5 cm] wide

24" [60 cm] of cord, $1/4$" [6 mm] in diameter

Matching sewing thread

Sewing box (see page 8)

Sewing machine

Size 16/100 (denim) machine needle

SIZE

Approximately $8^1/4$" x 12" [21 x 30 cm], excluding straps and handle

FABRIC CHOICE
If you can't find the right color of cotton tape, make two straps (see page 21) from one of the leftover fabrics.

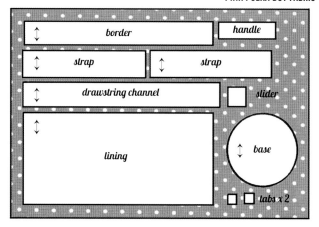

CUTTING OUT

FROM FLORAL FABRIC 1
- 28" x $10^3/4$" [70 x 27 cm] rectangle, for the main bag

FROM FLORAL FABRIC 2
- One outside flap (cut using template)

FROM FLORAL FABRIC 3
- One 9" [23 cm] circle, for the base

FROM PINK POLKA DOT FABRIC
- One 28" x $3^1/4$" [70 x 8 cm] border
- Two $17^3/4$" x 4" [45 x 10 cm] straps
- One 8" x $2^1/2$" [20 x 6 cm] handle
- One $28^1/4$" x $3^1/4$" [72 x 8 cm] drawstring channel
- One $27^1/2$" x $12^1/2$" [70 x 32 cm] lining
- One 9" [23 cm] circle, for the base
- One $3^1/4$" x $2^3/4$" [8 x 7 cm] slider
- Two 2" x 2" [5 x 5 cm] tabs

FROM RED POLKA DOT FABRIC
- One inside flap (from template)

FROM BATTING
- Two $17^1/4$" x $1^1/2$" [44 x 4 cm] strips, for the straps
- One $8^1/4$" [21 cm] circle, for the base

TAKE IT FURTHER

There's a real trend for backpacks at the moment, so if you're sewing this bag for an older child or for yourself, simply enlarge the pattern pieces for the main bag, base, and flap to make it a little bit larger.

TO MAKE THE BACKPACK

PREPARE THE BAG CYLINDER

Mark the center of the top edge of the main bag with a pin. Attach the recessed half of the magnetic fastener to the right side, $3^1/4$" [8 cm] below this point. With right sides together, pin and baste the pink polka dot border to the bottom edge. Machine stitch, taking a $3/8$" [1 cm] seam allowance, then press the seam allowance toward the border.

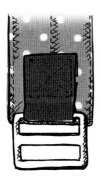

01 Pin the side edges together, matching the seam. Machine stitch, taking a $3/8$" [1 cm] allowance. Press the seam open. Turn right-side out and topstitch the other seam, $1/8$" [4 mm] from the edge of the border.

ASSEMBLE THE STRAPS

Press under a $3/8$" [1 cm] turning along the long edges and one end of a strap. Press in half widthwise. Slip the batting under the fold at one edge. Baste and topstitch the edges together. Stitch along the center.

02 Cut 4" [10 cm] of cotton tape and press a $3/8$" [1 cm] hem at one end. Slot through a buckle and baste the ends together. Sew across the tape, close to the buckle. Trim the raw end to $3/8$" [1 cm] and, with the folded end uppermost, baste and box stitch (see page 21) the tape to the turned-under end of the strap. Repeat for the second strap. With the buckles facing outward, pin and baste the raw ends to the top edge of the bag, $1^1/2$" [4 cm] from each side of the seam line.

SEW THE HANDLE

03 Fold the handle in half lengthwise, with right sides together. Pin and baste the long raw edge. Machine stitch, taking a $1/4$" [6 mm] seam allowance, then turn right-side out (see page 21). Press, then pin the ends to the top edge of the bag so that they overlap the inside edges of the straps by $3/8$" [1 cm].

PREPARE THE FLAP

04 Attach the second part of the fastener to the right side of the inside flap, $3/4$" [2 cm] up from the center bottom edge. With right sides together, pin and baste the side and bottom edges of the two flaps together. Machine stitch, taking a $1/4$" [6 mm] seam allowance. Clip the curves (see page 15) and turn right-side out. Press, then baste the top edges together. With right sides together, pin and baste the top edge to the bag so that it lies centrally over the straps and handle.

ADD THE DRAWSTRING CHANNEL

05 Baste the short ends of the strip together and machine stitch, taking a $3/4$" [2 cm] seam allowance. Leave a $3/8$" [1 cm] opening, $5/8$" [15 mm] from the bottom end of the seam, and reinforce the ends of the seam. Press the seam open, then press the strip in half lengthwise with the right-side outward. Baste the long edges together. With the opening in the seam lined up with the marker pin, and the raw edges aligned, pin and baste the channel around the top edge of the bag.

BASTE ON THE COTTON TAPE

06 Cut the remaining tape in half and make a double $3/8$" [1 cm] hem at one end of each piece. With right sides together, pin the raw ends to the bottom edge of the bag, 2" [5 cm] from each side of the seam.

PREPARE THE LINING

Baste the side edges of the lining with right sides together. Machine stitch, taking a $3/8$" [1 cm] seam, then press the seam open. Slip the lining over the bag, matching the seams, then pin and baste the top edges together. Using a denim needle, machine stitch twice through all the layers, $3/8$" [1 cm] from the edge. Turn the lining to the inside of the bag.

ADD THE BASE

07 Baste the circle of batting to the wrong side of the lining base. Pin the main-fabric base right-side up on top of the batting and baste around the outside edge. With the main-fabric base on the inside, pin and baste to the bottom edge of the bag. Sew in place, taking a $3/8$" [1 cm] seam allowance, as shown on page 15. Overlock or zigzag stitch the raw edges, then turn the bag right-side out. Thread the cotton tape through the buckles.

THREAD THE DRAWSTRING

08 Thread the cord through the drawstring channel. Press under a $3/8$" [1 cm] turning along the top and bottom edges of the slider. Unfold, then stitch along the side edges with right sides together, taking a $3/8$" [1 cm] seam allowance. Turn right-side out and fold the turnings to the inside. Stitch along the center of the tube and slot one cord through each side. Press under a $1/4$" [6 mm] turning along the top, bottom, and side edges of the tabs and hand stitch them to the ends of the cord.

04
05
06
07
08

BABY GIFT SET
BOTTLE HOLDER

There is a never-ending assortment of presents you can make for a newborn, but our very practical gift set—made up of this baby Bottle Holder, Terry-Cloth Bib, and Scallop-Edged Towel—has the benefit of being created out of a single large bath towel. Hone your bias-binding techniques on the bib and towel, and practice sewing a circle to a cylinder to make the bottle holder, which is the same basic structure as the Yoga Mat Bag and Gym Bag, just on a smaller scale. All three items are quick and easy to stitch.

MATERIALS & EQUIPMENT
18" x 12" [45 x 30 cm] of printed terry cloth
1¼ yards [1 m] of cotton tape, ¾" [2 cm] wide
4" x 4" [10 x 10 cm] of fusible adhesive web
4" x 4" [10 x 10 cm] of thick calico
Sewing thread to match tape
20" [50 cm] of cord, ¼" [6 mm] in diameter
Spring toggle
Adhesive tape
Safety pin
Sewing box (see page 8)
Sewing machine

SIZE
Approximately 8" tall x 4" [20 x 10 cm] in diameter

CUTTING OUT
FROM PRINTED TERRY CLOTH
- One 11¾" x 10¼" [30 x 26 cm] bag panel
- One 4" [10 cm] circle, for the base

FABRIC CHOICE
Any one—or all three—items would make a great present for a baby shower. They would also look very smart fitted into the Sport Bag (page 138), made in a coordinating print. Be sure to wash the towel before you start, to remove any fabric dressing that might irritate delicate skin.

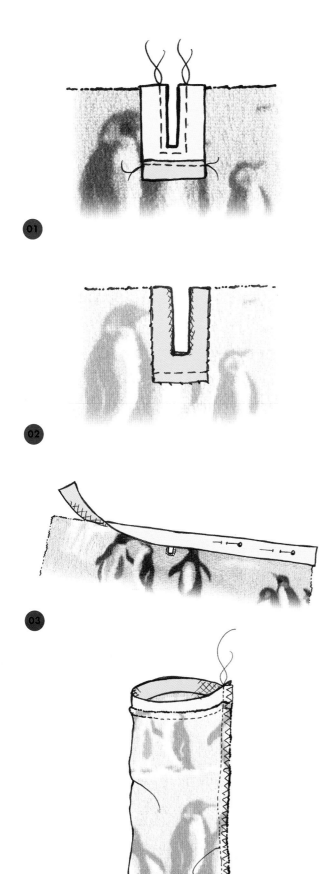

01

02

03

04

TO MAKE THE BOTTLE HOLDER

MAKE THE SLOT

01 Cut a 1¼" [3 cm] length of cotton tape and make a narrow single hem along one short end. With right sides together, pin the tape to the center top edge of the cover. Starting at the top, draw a ³/₄" [2 cm] line down the center of the tape with a fading fabric marker pen. Work a row of straight stitch ¹/₈" [4 mm] from each side of this line, sewing straight across the bottom end. Cutting ¹/₈" [4 mm] away from the stitches, carefully snip away the fabric within the seam line.

02 Turn the tape back through the opening and flatten it out on the wrong side of the terry cloth, so that you have a neat slot. Baste the edges of the tape to the terry cloth and slip-stitch in place.

ADD THE TAPE

03 Lay the cover right-side up on your work surface. Pin an 11³/₄" [30 cm] length of tape along the top edge. Baste it in place, then machine stitch, taking a ¹/₄" [6 mm] seam allowance. Press the seam allowance to one side, so that it lies across the tape.

SEW THE SIDE SEAM

04 Finish the side edges with a zigzag or overlocking stitch. With right sides together, fold the cover in half widthwise. Matching up the seam between the tape and the terry cloth, pin the two side edges together. Machine stitch, taking a ³/₈" [1 cm] seam allowance. Press the seam open.

MAKE THE GATHERING CHANNEL

05 Turn back the top of the cylinder so that the bottom edge of the tape lies ³/₄" [2 cm] below the folded edge. Pin in place, then slip-stitch the edge of the tape securely to the terry cloth.

REINFORCE THE BASE

Using a pair of compasses, draw a circle 3¹/₄" [8 cm] in diameter on the paper side of your fusible adhesive web. Following the manufacturer's instructions, press the adhesive side of the fusible web onto the calico, then cut out around the pencil line. Peel off the backing paper and press the adhesive side centrally onto the terry-cloth base.

PREPARE THE TAPE STRAP

06 Cut an $11^3/4$" [30 cm] length of tape and press it in half lengthwise, to give you a double layer, $3/8$" [1 cm] wide strap. Baste and stitch the outside edges together, then stitch the other long edge $1/8$" [4 mm] from the fold. Baste one end of the strap to the right side of the base, aligning the raw edges.

ATTACH THE BASE

07 With right sides together, pin the base to the bottom edge of the cylinder so that the strap is on the inside and its end lies centrally against the seam line (see page 15 for details of how to attach the base). Baste the two together, then machine stitch close to the edge of the calico. Sew over the end of the strap a couple of extra times to strengthen the join. Trim the seam allowance back to $1/4$" [6 mm] and finish the raw edges with a zigzag or overlocking stitch.

SECURE THE STRAP

Turn right-side out and ease out the base seam. Press under a $3/8$" [1 cm] turning at the loose end of the strap and stitch it securely to the top edge of the holder, just below the gathering channel.

ADD THE CORD

08 Wrap both ends of the cord tightly with adhesive tape. Fasten a safety pin to one end and feed it through the slot and around the gathering channel. Pass both ends of the cord through the spring toggle, then cut off the adhesive tape. Cut two $2^1/2$" [6 cm] lengths from the remaining cotton tape and press under a narrow turning at one end of each piece. With the wrong side facing inward, baste the raw end of one piece of tape to one end of the cord. Wrap it around the cord several times, then slip-stitch down the folded edge. Sew the top and bottom edges together to make a cushion-shaped tab. Finish off the other end of the cord in the same way.

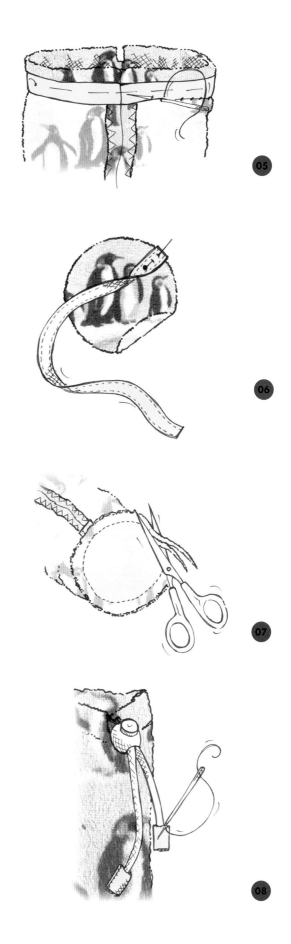

05

06

07

08

TERRY-CLOTH BIB

Babies get through several clean bibs every day, so you could always make a stack of these to welcome a new arrival.

MATERIALS & EQUIPMENT

TEMPLATE ON PAGES 156–157

12" x 16" [30 x 40 cm] of printed terry cloth
1³/₄ yards [160 cm] of bias binding, ¹/₂" [12 mm] wide
Sewing thread to match binding
One hook-and-loop tape circle, ³/₄" [1 cm] in diameter, or one large snap
Sewing box (see page 8)
Sewing machine

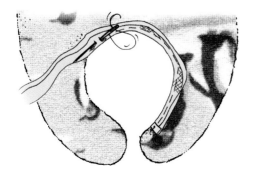

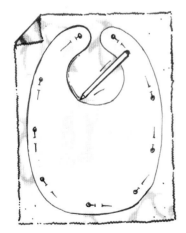

SIZE

10¹/₄" x 14¹/₄" [26 x 36 cm]

TO MAKE THE BIB

CUT OUT THE BIB

01 Trace the bib template on page 156 onto a large sheet of paper and cut it out. Pin it to the wrong side of the terry cloth, then draw around the outside edge with a fading fabric marker pen. Cut out, carefully following the drawn line.

BIND THE EDGE

You can find detailed instructions on applying bias binding to curved edges on page 17.

02 Start at the point marked A on the template, on the inside of the left strip. Open out the right-hand fold of the binding, then make a ¹/₄" [6 mm] turning at the end. Baste the open fold around the neck, lining the edge up with the edge of the bib, then continue all the way around the outer edge. When you get back to the beginning, trim the end down to ³/₈" [1 cm] and tuck it behind the fold. Machine stitch the binding to the bib, following the open fold line as precisely as you can.

Turn the binding to the back of the bib, so that the raw edge is enclosed. Baste it in place, then slip-stitch the folded edge in line with the machine stitches.

ADD THE FASTENING

03 Separate the two halves of the hook-and-loop tape circle or the snap. Sew the looped half of the hook-and-loop tape or the recessed half of the snap to the top of the left strap and the remaining half in the corresponding position on the underside of the right strap.

TAKE IT FURTHER

You can personalize the bib by adding the baby's name. Write directly on the fabric with a fading fabric marker pen, and embroider over the letters in chain stitch (see page 18).

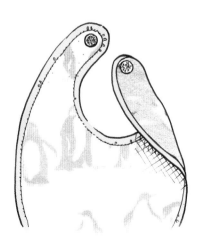

03

Baby Gift Set 151

SCALLOP-EDGED TOWEL

Inspired by a well-worn and much-loved vintage original, the softly curved ends give this rectangular baby towel a special appeal.

MATERIALS & EQUIPMENT

TEMPLATE ON PAGE 155

$26^{1}/_{4}$" x $35^{1}/_{2}$" [65 x 90 cm] rectangle of printed terry cloth
$4^{1}/_{2}$ yards [4 m] of bias binding, $^{1}/_{2}$" [12 mm] wide
Sewing thread to match binding
Sewing box (see page 8)
Sewing machine

SIZE

$26^{1}/_{4}$" x $34^{3}/_{4}$" [65 x 88 cm]

TO MAKE THE TOWEL

DRAW ON THE SCALLOPS

Trace the scallop template on page 155 and cut it out. Lay the terry cloth rectangle on your work surface with the wrong side facing upward. Pin the template to the bottom left corner, matching the straight edges. Draw inside the curve and along the right-hand edge with a fading fabric marker pen.

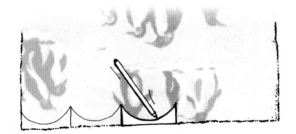

01 Remove the template and repin it next to the first curve, so that the left edge is lined up with the vertical line. Once again, draw inside the curve and the along the right-hand edge. Repeat this three more times, then draw five more scallops along the other short end in the same way. Cut carefully along both wavy lines.

BIND THE EDGE

02 With the right side of the towel facing you, baste the bias binding all the way around the outside, starting with a straight edge. Be sure to turn under the end of the binding at the end of the round and cover the beginning end with it. You will need to make a little pleat at each inside corner, but you can find detailed instructions for how to deal with curves on page 17. Machine stitch the binding in place and turn it over to the back. Baste, then slip-stitch the folded edge.

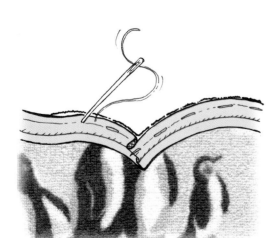

TEMPLATES
SIZE: 100%

WINDOW FRAME

LUGGAGE TAG
(pages 115 to 117)

EYE MASK POUCH (pages 78 to 81)
TASSEL

STITCHING LINE

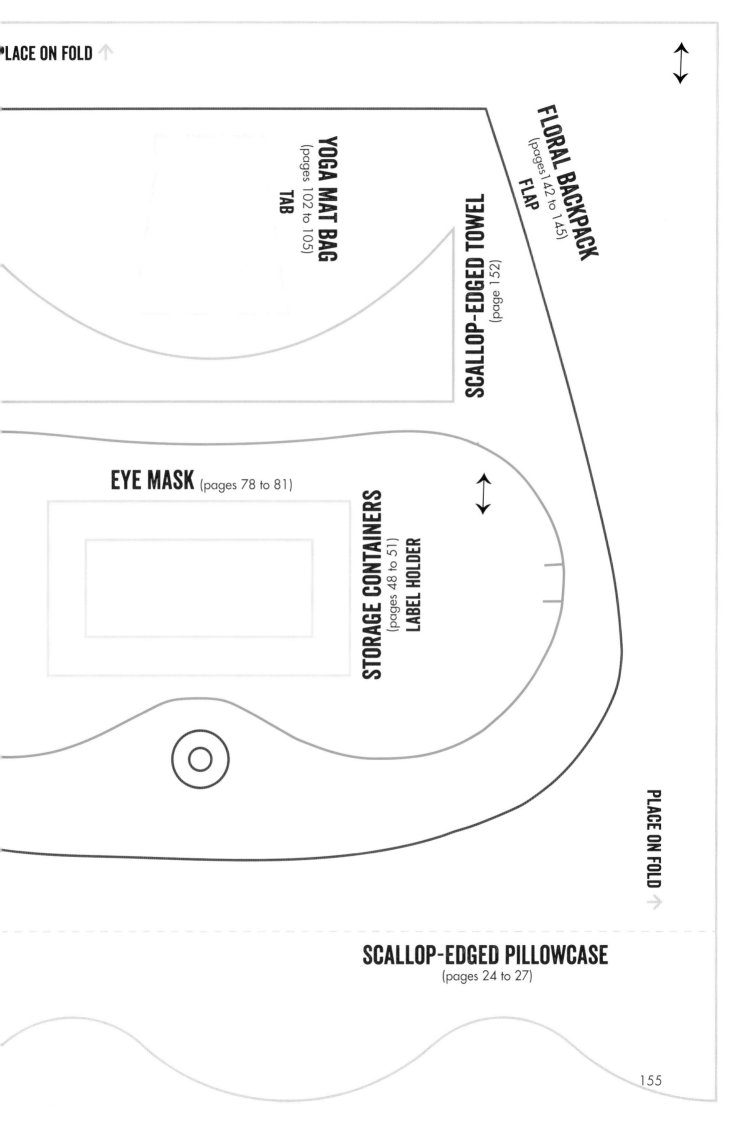

FLORAL BACKPACK
(pages 142 to 145)
FLAP

YOGA MAT BAG
(pages 102 to 105)
TAB

SCALLOP-EDGED TOWEL
(page 152)

EYE MASK (pages 78 to 81)

STORAGE CONTAINERS
(pages 48 to 51)
LABEL HOLDER

PLACE ON FOLD →

SCALLOP-EDGED PILLOWCASE
(pages 24 to 27)

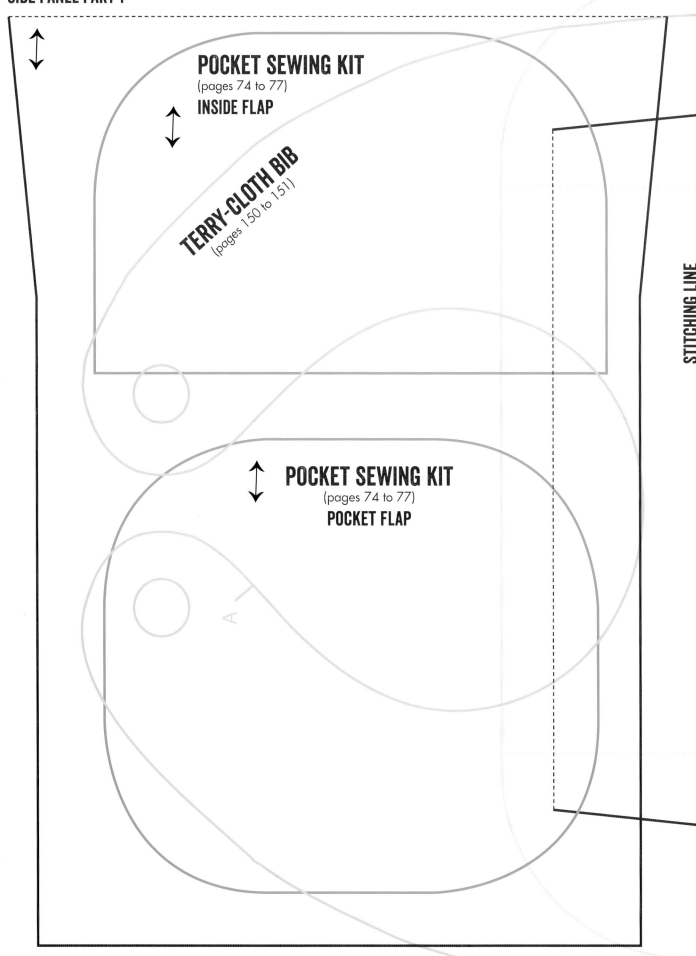

POCKET SEWING KIT
(pages 74 to 77)
INSIDE FLAP

TERRY-CLOTH BIB
(pages 150 to 151)

POCKET SEWING KIT
(pages 74 to 77)
POCKET FLAP

STITCHING LINE

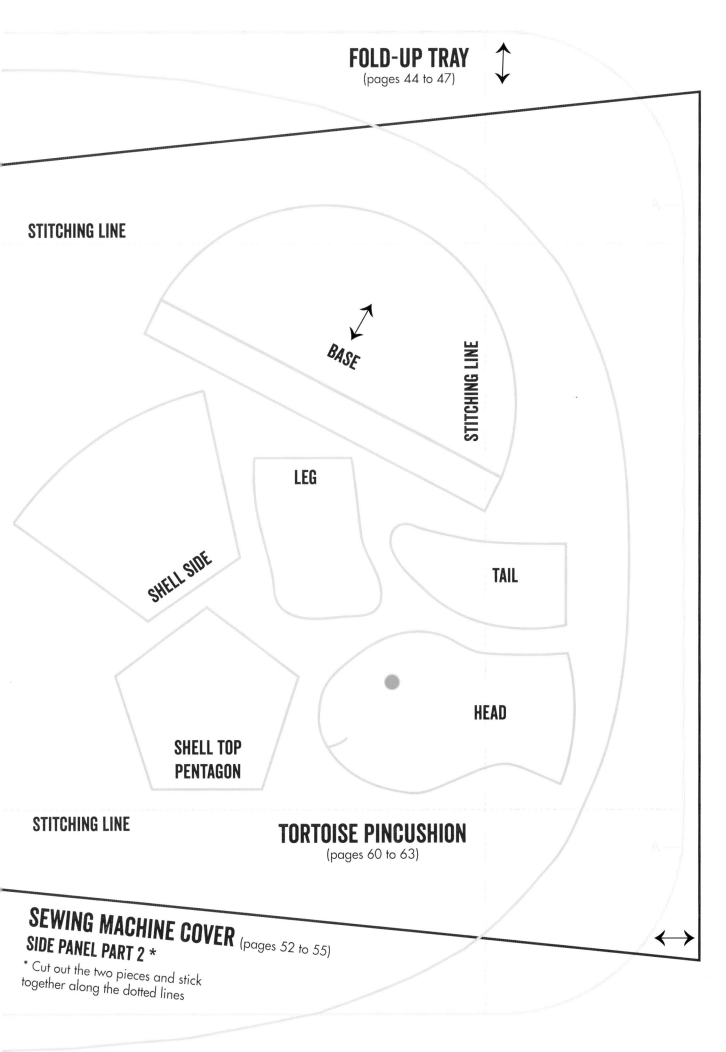

FOLD-UP TRAY
(pages 44 to 47)

STITCHING LINE

BASE

STITCHING LINE

LEG

SHELL SIDE

TAIL

HEAD

SHELL TOP
PENTAGON

STITCHING LINE

TORTOISE PINCUSHION
(pages 60 to 63)

SEWING MACHINE COVER (pages 52 to 55)
SIDE PANEL PART 2 *

* Cut out the two pieces and stick
together along the dotted lines

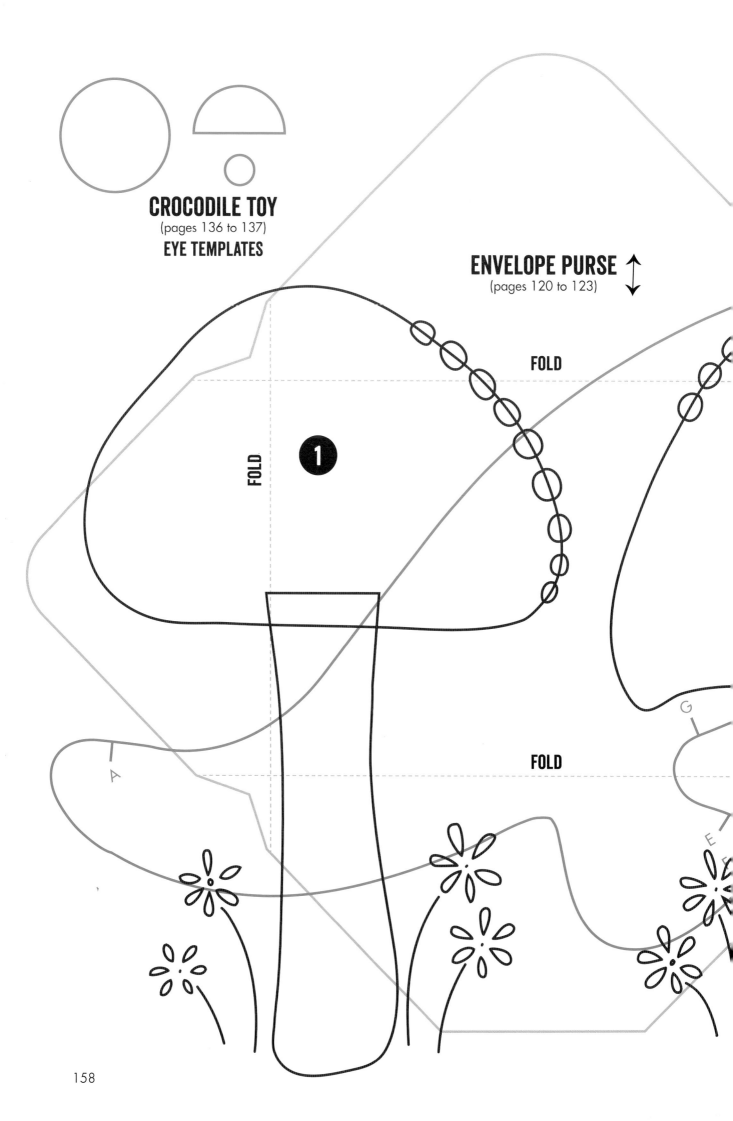

CROCODILE TOY
(pages 136 to 137)
EYE TEMPLATES

ENVELOPE PURSE ↕
(pages 120 to 123)

FOLD

FOLD

FOLD

1

A

G

E

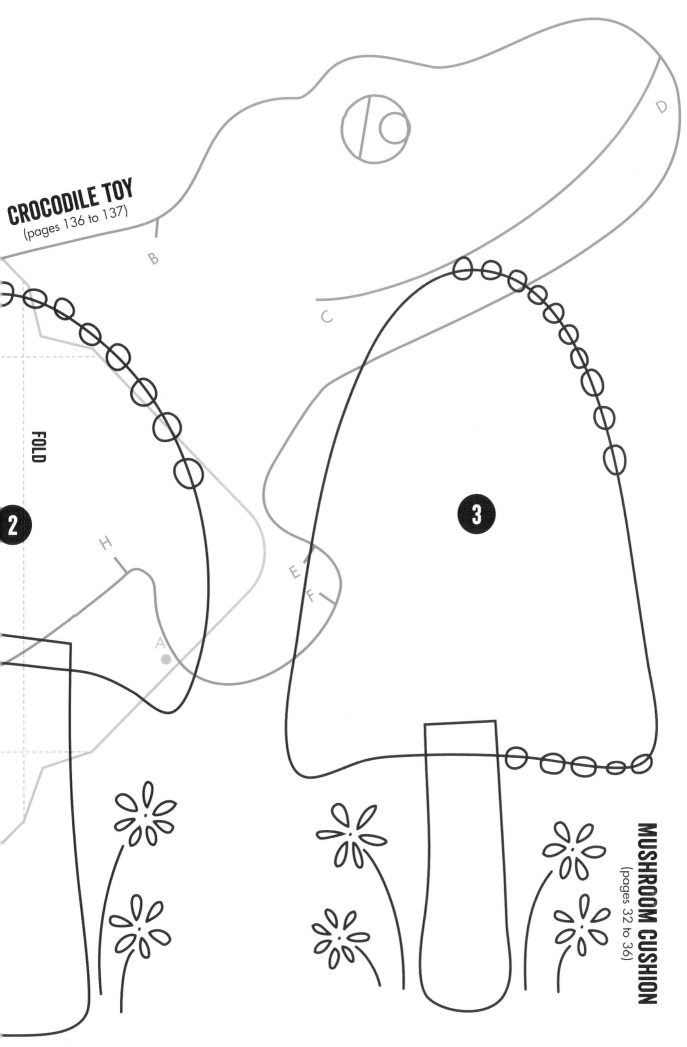

CROCODILE TOY
(pages 136 to 137)

B

C

D

FOLD

H

E

F

A

2

3

MUSHROOM CUSHION
(pages 32 to 36)

RESOURCES

For Cath Kidston fabrics, visit cathkidston.com. The lightweight cotton fabrics are called "haberdashery fabric."

For pattern paper, use quilter's graph paper available from quilting supplies stores, or visit vintagevisage.co.uk for 36-inch-wide cross-and-dot paper, which has marks every inch.

For spring clips for the Glasses Case (page 70), contact u-handbag.com.

CATH'S ACKNOWLEDGMENTS

My special thanks to everyone involved in the making of this book: to Lucinda Ganderton for making the projects, Elaine Ashton, Jessica Pemberton, and Luciana Sly at Cath Kidston Ltd. To Rita Platts for the photography, and to Anne Furniss, Helen Lewis, Nikki Dupin, and Zelda Turner at Quadrille.

CREATIVE COORDINATOR: Elaine Ashton
HEAD CREATIVE RESEARCHER TO CATH KIDSTON:
Jessica Pemberton
CREATIVE RESEARCH ASSISTANT: Luciana Sly

EDITORIAL DIRECTOR: Anne Furniss
CREATIVE DIRECTOR: Helen Lewis
PROJECTS,INSTRUCTIONS & ILLUSTRATIONS PREPARED BY:
Lucinda Ganderton
PROJECT EDITOR: Zelda Turner
ART DIRECTOR: Nikki Dupin
DESIGNER: Emma Wells
PHOTOGRAPHER: Rita Platts
STYLIST: Holly Bruce
SEWING ASSISTANT: Anna Stefaniak
PRODUCTION DIRECTOR: Vincent Smith
PRODUCTION CONTROLLER: Aysun Hughes

10 9 8 7 6 5 4 3 2 1

First published in 2014 by Quadrille Publishing Limited www.quadrille.co.uk

Quadrille is an imprint of Hardie Grant www.hardiegrant.com.au

Text copyright © Cath Kidston 2014
Design templates and projects © Cath Kidston 2014
Photography © Rita Platts
Design and layout copyright © Quadrille Publishing Limited 2014

Thanks to Hobbycraft (www.hobbycraft.co.uk) for sewing room props and accessories, to Brother (www.brothersewing.co.uk) for the loan of the Brother sewing machine, and to Winter's Moon (www.wintersmoon.co.uk) for the gray formica table.

Cataloguing-in-Publication Data: a catalogue record for this book is available from the British Library.

ISBN: 978 184949 667 4

Printed in China